D0285349

DISCARD

The Predator Next Door
Detect, Protect and Recover from Betrayal

* * *

By Darlene Ellison, M.S.

HTA Books
High Touch Alliances
2634 Lakeforest Court
Dallas, Texas 75214

Visit our website at www.thepredatornextdoor.com

ISBN: 978-0-9822864-0-1 - $14.95

This book is dedicated to my two amazing children, Austin and Alexa. Everybody needs a hero, and I am fortunate enough to have two. Hold your heads high, be yourselves, help others and follow your dreams.

And remember, *there is no box.*

TABLE OF CONTENTS

The Journey Home

THE JOURNEY HOME

Home.

*Thinking, trying to figure out how to get home; I concentrate, yet
nothing comes to mind. I do not know how to get there yet.*

*Looking toward home to find the answer to my grief;
I squint, but cannot see.
Reaching my arms toward home to find solutions to my pain;
I grasp at thin air to no avail.*

*Doing all I can to find my home; I am told that it is
my secret source of strength.
Thinking, looking, reaching, doing... STOP!*

*Be still and listen.
Stop moving and stand still. Breathe deeply. Listen... what is
that sound? It is a tiny voice calling me home. I am still and I am
listening—I think I understand.*

*The journey home is a process, filled with milestones and lessons.
My journey is enriched by my faith in Him and the support of
those I encounter along the path.*

*My home is sacred, as is yours. We all have a home. Some are
rooms without doors; others have doors of steel
with complicated locks.*

*My home is where He lives.
Home is a peaceful place where I dwell in faith, hope,
determination and strength.*

*As I near my most peaceful home, I see the gifts so clearly.
Even in the depths of darkness, the glimmer of silver
linings shines brightly.*

*At home, I am a jewel. I am one of many in the world,
yet my markings, my journey home are uniquely mine.
At home, I am extraordinary.*

*At home, I do not merely survive—I thrive.
I have found my way. The path reveals itself gradually.*

I'm coming home.

PROLOGUE

MY HUSBAND, THE PREDATOR

On February 12, 2005, I was hit by a train. No, it was not an actual train. But the sudden impact was just as startling and powerful. I didn't hear the whistle. I didn't feel the ground rumbling beneath my feet. I didn't even know that I was standing on the tracks. Without warning, this train exploded my life into a million fragments.

In the ensuing weeks, if you had met me on the street, you never would have mistaken me for a victim. I looked like the typical busy mom with two beautiful children. My professional background includes a former practice in psychology and counseling, followed by assignments as a consultant and a business development officer in a community bank. I was the owner of a cozy home on a quiet street, in the same neighborhood where I was raised and my family still lives. Sure, my little family had typical difficulties and went through its share of hard times. But a disaster was not even a possibility, I thought.

Then the train roared through our happy lives, and everything changed forever. My world – and more importantly, my children's world – was plunged into paralyzing darkness and chaos.

There in that darkness, in the pitch-black pain of my soul, I found a light. I found hope. I found transformation. And my real journey began.

I have written this book because it lives inside of me. This story is my and my children's story. It does not define us. Instead, it has served as a catalyst for us to grow and reach out to others. It outlines my incredible journey from the darkness of betrayal into the light of transformation.

This book is more than a story telling how I survived an unimaginable, horrific series of events. It is more than a heart-wrenching account of secret lives, pain and betrayal.

This is a book about hope, determination and finding strength in the face of monstrous adversity. It can protect children from dangerous predators by informing parents, grandparents and other caretakers. Plus, it can provide a guide for those who wish to survive – and thrive – after any kind of betrayal, whether physical, emotional or both.

This is my conversation with the broken-hearted, the lost, the sad, and anyone who has ever had the rug pulled out from under him or her. Take my hand, stand up and brush yourself off. May you be empowered to move through your journey with grace, peace and, ultimately, joy.

SECTION 1

A PREDATOR
LURKS NEARBY

You may encounter many defeats, but you must not be defeated. In fact, it may be necessary to encounter the defeats, so you can know who you are, what you can rise from, how you can still come out of it.

–Maya Angelou

CHAPTER | 1

AN AUSPICIOUS BEGINNING

His ocean-blue eyes were impossible to miss.

As I sat in the country club dining room, I couldn't help but steal a glance at the new guy in town. This handsome young dentist in his early 30s had just purchased an established dental practice in my hometown of Lakewood, a small upscale Dallas community. Now Todd Calvin was working the room, trying to drum up business at a social event sponsored by the chamber of commerce.

My father, a local banker, was president of the organization. Dad had heard my frequent complaints that I was the last single woman in the community. So when Todd joined the chamber of commerce and joked that he was looking for a "house and a spouse," Dad responded, "I can probably help you with both."

At the time, I was a well-grounded young woman with big dreams, including a fulfilling career. After completing a master's degree in psychology, I became a licensed psychological associate. I joined my mother, a licensed guidance counselor, in a growing private practice. Together, we established a complete educational center offering assessments, counseling and tutoring to children and adolescents. I specialized in helping children ages 4 through 12 with behavior modification, while assisting their families with a variety of issues. At the same time, I spent hours working toward my doctorate degree.

When we met at the country club, Todd looked like the total package. He was nice-looking, ambitious, and had big plans for the future. Within weeks, it became clear he had set his sights on me. We soon fell into a dating routine reminiscent of the 1950s. On Thursday, he would call to ask for a weekend date. We would spend Friday or Saturday night together on outings that were conventional and even old-fashioned. During these dates, we quickly found common ground – a mutual love for music and singing, as well as a long history of volunteering and working with children.

I was drawn in by Todd's seemingly generous spirit. He had gained a good reputation as a camp counselor and youth leader at a neighborhood church. One of his greatest aspirations was to fly his own airplane, which would allow him to ferry underprivileged sick children to hospitals for much-needed medical treatment.

Todd longed for a big family. His career was taking off. On paper, he was the man I had dreamed about. Todd swept me off my feet.

For our six-month dating anniversary, we spent a weekend away at the beach. Todd hinted at a future together, and my heart soared. He was Prince Charming, and he actually wanted me. For the first time, I blurted out, "I love you."

I decided that my life was, in fact, a fairy tale. Todd was a white knight, and I was a princess.

I was clinging to these dreams when my birthday rolled around in August of 1992. Todd requested that I dress to the nines for a special date celebrating the occasion. As I readied myself for the evening, I could hardly contain my excitement. I was convinced that, by night's end, I would have an engagement ring on my finger.

Promptly at 7 p.m., a dashing Todd arrived to pick me up. A short drive took us to the Mansion on Turtle Creek, long considered one of the city's toniest restaurants. The hostess and waiters addressed Todd by name, with greetings of, "Good evening, Dr. Calvin." I was enamored by the attention. Imagine a husband who is well-known even at the finest establishments, I thought.

Todd clearly relished the impression he was making. His coy smiles hinted that he knew a secret, but refused to tell. The growing excitement and mystery began to take their toll. My nerves prevented me from enjoying the fabulous food. I looked everywhere for signs, disappointed when the only thing at the bottom of my glass was wine. There was no ring in sight.

As our dinner neared its conclusion, I finally sat back, sighed and relaxed. It was not to be, I thought to myself. This was nothing more than a lovely dinner to celebrate my birthday. The waiter asked if we would like dessert, and I politely declined. I just wanted to go home and be miserable by myself.

Todd had other plans. "Come on, honey, let's have a little birthday dessert," he said.

"No, thanks," I answered. "I simply couldn't eat another bite."

His tone changed, taking on a note of urgency. I detected a furtive glance between Todd and the waiter, whose face betrayed a slight tinge of panic. "Well, I would like some dessert, and you can share it," Todd said. The waiter bustled away, leaving me uncomfortable and confused.

About two minutes later, the restaurant was filled with chuckles. A legion of waiters swarmed throughout the dining room, delivering a box of Cracker Jack to each table. Todd commanded attention, ensuring that his intended bride was center stage. I tore open the box to find an amazing prize – a stunning diamond solitaire engagement ring that exceeded my wildest expectations.

My eyes filled with tears as the handsome, intelligent man of my dreams fell before me on one knee. He very simply asked me to marry him. My cry of "yes" echoed through the room, and our rapt audience applauded. Indeed, my life had become a fairy tale.

I threw myself into the wedding, determined that it would be a perfect start to our perfect life together. My mother, sister and I embarked on a whirlwind of dress shopping, bridal showers and portraits. The wedding ballooned into a 500-guest affair, with 16 attendants and two priests officiating at my childhood cathedral – the very church where my parents had married decades before. The pending nuptials of the singing dentist and his psychologist fiancée even garnered media attention. Our courtship and upcoming wedding were featured in *The Dallas Morning News*, which raised the stakes in my mind. This had to turn out right.

I nurtured dreams of a large house, a country-club membership and motherhood. I planned to work as a consultant, with a flexible schedule that would enable me to put our children first. We would have a lake house, a boat ... the possibilities were endless.

The countdown was on. A week before the wedding, I awakened to a shock. Tiny blisters covered my body inside and out. Chickenpox! Exhausted from a high fever and itching that made sleep impossible, I refused my doctor's suggestion to postpone the wedding. I was determined to forge ahead, though I spent an uncomfortable week in tears. One friend joked that perhaps my illness was a bad omen or a sign from God. I hurriedly pushed the suggestion aside as a ridiculous superstition. Only now, years later, do I wonder if there was truth in this statement.

At last, the wedding arrived. On April 24, 1993, Todd and I were married. He whisked me off to Maui – the perfect honeymoon for a fairy-tale princess. On the second day of our trip, we talked about the future.

"I have always wanted to be a private pilot," Todd said. "Since I was a little boy, I've wanted to own an airplane. Wouldn't it be great if we could make that happen in just a couple of years? I'd like to start flying lessons soon."

I hesitated. When I was a child, a neighbor died in a private-plane crash. The memory haunted me.

"Honey, to be honest, that really scares me," I said softly, telling him about my childhood trauma. "If something happened to you, I don't know what I would do."

I expected a calm discussion. At the least, I thought my husband would comfort me, assuring me that he would take extensive lessons. Instead, he sneered at me in disgust. Almost immediately, a coolness swept between us.

"Maybe this was a mistake," Todd said. "Maybe I shouldn't have married you."

Shock overcame me. Could such a small disagreement turn my husband against me so completely? At the time, I was determined to create a fairy-tale marriage with this wonderfully successful man. I overlooked Todd's insensitivity and other faults, convinced they were minor aberrations.

Now, years later, I see the reality of the situation. I simply did not know Todd Calvin at all.

CHAPTER | 2
SIGNS OF TROUBLE

When we returned from the honeymoon, it was time to experience real life together as husband and wife. I set up housekeeping in Todd's tiny home in Mesquite, a less-expensive suburb several miles from his dental practice.

We both worked hard. I was still in private practice with my mother, while also in the middle of my doctoral program, and Todd was at the office from sunup until sundown. He experienced frustration typical for a young dentist, since he put in long hours but did not yet have the money or possessions to show for his troubles. I played the role of a loyal and supportive wife, helping him concoct marketing ideas and other strategies to build his dreamed-of, million-dollar practice.

I desperately wanted us to become a team, creating a wonderful life together. Yet our physical relationship – or lack thereof – deeply hurt and disappointed me. When we began dating, Todd was a perfect gentleman. He made no physical advances until deep into our courtship. I jokingly asked if he was gay. "No, I'm just an old-fashioned guy," he answered reassuringly.

Even after our marriage, we lacked chemistry. I told myself not to worry about it. After all, that kind of passion was the stuff of books and movies, not real life. I needed to focus on making this relationship work – with or without chemistry.

We settled into a weekly routine that culminated in Friday-night fights. Almost every Friday evening ended in a brief argument, followed by a weekend of silence. This increased the physical distance between us, and I filled my days with work and studying. We both tried to keep up some semblance of a marriage. Within a year, I was pregnant. Todd was elated at the news. At last, we had a bond that would bring us closer together, I thought.

Aglow with excitement, I began shopping for the nursery. I also embarked on the typical schedule of doctor visits. After my first sonogram, the obstetrician called us into his office.

"I have some minor concerns about your baby's development," the doctor said. "I'm going to refer you to a neonatal specialist."

We pressed the doctor for more information, and at last he relented. There was no way to be sure just yet, he said. But it could be Down syndrome. Several more tests revealed no conclusive diagnosis. Our baby boy might have a challenging medical condition – or he might be perfectly normal. We simply didn't know.

I was tortured by the unknown. I irrationally began to review every piece of food I had put in my mouth and every drop of liquid that had passed my lips. What had I done to cause this? What were the chances he would be healthy? What should we do next?

I was now in the second trimester and looking for answers. An amniocentesis might reveal more about our baby's condition, our doctor explained, but it could put his health at risk so late in the pregnancy. We had to make a decision fast. Did we want to undergo this test?

That evening, Todd and I weighed the pros and cons of amniocentesis.

"I know there is some risk," I said. "but I have to know – definitively – whether he has Down syndrome. If he does, I want to be prepared. I can do research before he is born and understand how to best deal with the situation."

Todd agreed that I should undergo the test. In fact, he was adamant. But not for the same reasons.

"I have no intention of raising a child with any sort of birth defect or deformity," Todd said, seeming almost pleased with himself. "We have to do the amniocentesis as soon as possible. If the baby has Down syndrome, I've found a doctor in Kansas who will take care of things."

"What do you mean, take care of things?" I asked, cringing at the answer I assumed would follow.

"An abortion," Todd said, in a matter-of-fact tone. "He does late-term abortions. We might have a harder time finding a doctor around here who would help us out."

The room fell silent as I stared at this man. I could not believe my ears. Surely, I had misunderstood.

"You've got to be joking," I said. "I would never have an abortion. I love this baby, no matter what."

"Look," Todd retorted. "It's very simple. If this baby has Down syndrome, I'm gone. I will not stay married to you, and I will not raise a kid with problems. End of discussion."

For the next several days, I silently went through the motions of living. My mind was at war with itself, refusing to believe the ultimatum my husband had delivered. This man, who was supposed to be my loving partner, was demanding that I abandon my deepest and most cherished beliefs. I made a conscious decision to keep my worries, pain and feelings of betrayal to myself. I put on some rose-colored glasses, pasted a fake smile on my face, and decided to just get along. I pretended that our devastating conversation had never happened.

We moved forward with the amniocentesis and awaited the results. The evening after the test, we gathered at my parents' home for dinner. Todd's parents had driven all the way from Arkansas to show their support. We gathered around the table in silence. My swollen face and stuffy nose were the result of hours of crying. My baby's grandparents believed that I was grieving for a child who might face a difficult life. They didn't know the truth. In fact, I was heartbroken that I might have to choose between my marriage and my baby – and I already knew that my baby would win.

After dinner, Todd's mother took me aside. Her red-rimmed eyes showed that she had been crying as well. I expected a hug and some reassurance. Instead, I received a shock when she took me firmly by the shoulders.

"Please, no matter how the tests turn out, I'm begging you not to kill this baby," she pleaded with her eyes locked onto mine.

"Todd has spent his entire life dreaming of fatherhood. It would destroy him if you got an abortion. Please don't do this to him."
Nausea swept over me, and the room began to sway. I fled to the bathroom, my head spinning. What had Todd told his parents? Was he setting the stage for me to be the villain who killed his baby if the test results were not what he had hoped? I prayed fervently for the health of my son – not just for my baby's sake, but also so Todd would not leave me.

On July 21, 1994, Austin Calvin was born, a healthy baby boy. Todd was at my side.

* * *

I embraced motherhood. Todd's dental practice was still in the red. So, in addition to raising my son, I had to continue working. My dissertation was put on the back burner.

While Todd and I built a life together, our relationship still felt empty. I longed for another child, hoping this would be the cure for our marriage. Just shy of two years after Austin's birth, our daughter Alexa arrived.

As Todd's practice began to succeed financially, I was able to work less and focus more on my favorite job: being a mom. I went to work as a development consultant for schools and non-profit organizations. This allowed me to set my own schedule, so I was always available to ferry the kids to T-ball and soccer practices, or to volunteer at the school carnival.

Together, our little family shared good times and a great deal of laughter. These sunny moments, however, always involved the children. Conversations between Todd and me centered on three topics: the kids, the dental practice and the things Todd wanted to buy now that his business was making money. Our fights became almost non-existent. Why should we fight when we hardly spoke?

As the money flowed, we built a new home in Lakewood, just minutes from my family, our church and Todd's dental practice. Despite his lifelong claims that he dreamed of fatherhood, Todd's life became consumed with fun and games – away from the family. Ignoring my concerns, Todd became a licensed private pilot and began looking for a plane to buy "for the family." The idea of owning a plane horrified me. I was haunted by irrational images of losing my entire family in one crash. Todd proceeded anyway and invested in a plane.

One weekend, Todd went to a boat show and came home with a large sailboat. Neither of us knew how to sail. In fact, he had never even mentioned wanting to own a sailboat. He saw it, wanted it and bought it – without consulting me.

He spent weekends on his sailboat or flying to exotic destinations. Occasionally, when schedules allowed, the kids and I spent time with him on the boat or attended events held by a club of private-plane owners called the Flying Dentists. I still feared small planes, however, and was content to stay home most of the time.

From 2001 through 2003, Todd travelled continually. He received special training to fly over mountains and oceans. This was followed by trips all over the world, from Canada and Cuba to Grand Cayman and the Turks and Caicos Islands. Often, he would fly out on a Wednesday evening or Thursday morning and not return until Sunday night. I would sigh with relief, make plans with the kids for the weekend, and then cry myself to sleep for living in this sham of a marriage.

As Todd became more enraptured with travel and spent more time away from home, he became less engaged in the children's everyday activities and sports. He seemed to be leaving his Christian faith behind as well. Our lives became completely separate, other than sharing a bed when he was in town. Even when Todd was home, he would spend long hours on the computer, behind closed doors. His email was password-protected. Whenever I entered the room unannounced, he would quickly close whatever he had been working on.

Todd's business had become the million-dollar practice of his dreams. Throughout the city, he was affectionately known as the "singing dentist." He serenaded his patients, especially on their birthdays, to build a feeling of caring and trust. Todd encouraged parents to bring their children into the practice, where he made everyone comfortable with his wit and charm. "We love kids" was a slogan that could be found on his ads.

By all outward appearances, we were the perfect

family with the perfect life. We had a nice home. We travelled. We had an airplane and a boat. Our children excelled at their parochial school.

Behind closed doors, Todd's behavior became increasingly upsetting. He avoided socializing and didn't have an identifiable circle of friends. He began to express aggressive, negative opinions on sensitive societal issues and share them with whomever would listen.

Todd also began picking me apart. He would react defensively to just about any statement I made. During our last five years together, he regaled me with derogatory comments about women in general – and about me specifically. To Todd, I was fat, stupid and brought nothing of value to our marriage. He was the successful dentist, and I was dead weight. He should just divorce me and get it over with. Despite his hateful diatribes, I kept trying.

In May 2003, I agreed to hang up my hat as a consultant. I would spend the summer with the kids, and then come to work for Todd in his practice in the fall. I already had kept his books for years. He felt that having me at the front desk, with all of my community involvement and marketing background, would help drive the practice to be even more successful than in previous years. I gave notice to the organizations for which I was working and prepared to start my job with Todd on the Tuesday after Labor Day. Surely, this would save my marriage.

Just a month later, our relationship had deteriorated to a new low. One day in early July, our family was gathered in the kitchen. Todd lost his temper and began screaming at me, his hand raised in a threatening pose as our children looked on in shock.

"I am through with you. I want a divorce," he shouted.

At long last, I had enough. I had done all that I knew to do to save this marriage. Without a moment's hesitation, I quietly conceded, "You've got it."

The divorce was over in just 60 days. Despite their rapid progression, those two months were confusing, belligerent and just plain crazy at times. Todd's irrational opinions on society kept popping up in bizarre ways. He did not want custody of the children, yet vowed to take them on his airplane whenever and wherever he wished. He was going to fight paying alimony, declaring, "You came into this marriage making $30,000 a year, and you'll leave this marriage making not a penny more."

Late one night, Todd sat down at our kitchen table and wrote a long letter describing "all the reasons you make me want to vomit." He threatened to "go to another country, leaving my parents and family behind, to avoid having to pay you another penny."

Oddly enough, he was proud of this letter. He waved it around and quoted from it the next morning, then left it on the counter for me to read in its entirety. I copied it, hiding the copy for safekeeping. Little did I know that just 15 months later, that letter might have saved our lives.

CHAPTER | 3

A PEDOPHILE IN OUR MIDST

Saturday, February 12, 2005

I woke with a chill. On that ordinary February day, Dallas was blanketed with gray clouds and spattered with intermittent drizzle that threatened to glaze the streets with ice.

The gloomy weather prompted a lazy Saturday morning of pajamas, pancakes and cartoons with the kids. Glancing over my calendar, I planned to stop by the yoga studio where I was an instructor and marketing coordinator, followed by an evening at a local charity auction. Life seemed so normal that day. Yet within a few short hours, my slight morning chill would be transformed into cold, hard fear.

I headed to the yoga studio to put in a quick hour of work. A few minutes at the front-desk computer were followed by a chat with my boss about marketing ideas. When my mobile phone rang, I was tempted to ignore the unfamiliar number that popped up on caller ID. But something made me answer.

The young man on the other end of the line said he worked for a home security company. The alarm had gone off at the house of my ex-husband, Todd, he said. The security company was unable to reach him.

Immediately, I was perplexed and agitated. The divorce had

been finalized 15 months ago. Why had Todd left my name as the emergency contact for the alarm company?

"Ma'am?" the young man prodded. "Do you have any other numbers where we might reach Dr. Calvin?"

I reeled off every phone number I knew for Todd, from his mobile phone to his pager and office number. I was tempted to simply hang up but hesitated for a moment.

"Have the police been called?" I asked.

"Yes, ma'am, the police are en route," the young man explained. "When we called Dr. Calvin's residence to verify the alarm, someone answered and identified himself as a special agent with the Dallas division of the FBI."

As I hung up the phone, I was completely bewildered. Questions raced through my mind. Was this some kind of joke? What had Todd done? Where was he?

My fingers began working on autopilot, pressing the buttons of my mobile phone. I tried every method of contacting Todd, leaving increasingly angry voicemails at each step. I needed to know what was happening. And there was only one way to find out.

When I pulled up in front of Todd's house, it was like being transported to the set of a crime drama. Two police squad cars sat by the curb, while an unfamiliar blue van and a small dark car were parked in the driveway. A handful of neighbors gathered across the street to gawk, while eyes peeked out from behind the curtains and blinds of the house next door. As I sat idling at the curb, at least six investigators wearing surgical gloves carried boxes and computers from Todd's house to the van.

The chill within me deepened, freezing me to the driver's seat of the car. A dozen scenarios flew through my mind. Had Todd been arrested for tax evasion? Was he smuggling drugs in his private plane? What was he hiding? Or could this simply be a case of mistaken identity?

My reverie was broken by a tall, blond woman wearing a blue FBI windbreaker.

"Are you the ex-wife?" she asked.

After my hesitant answer, she escorted me to the front porch and asked me to wait. My stomach began to ache as the fear grew in my belly. At last, a kind yet serious face emerged from the house. Special Agent Michael Call asked if I knew what was happening. When I answered with a shake of my head, he asked me to come into the house and answer a few questions.

As I sank into the handsome leather couch in Todd's living room, the cold seeped into my fingers and toes. I began to shiver, even as Agent Call asked that I not touch anything in the house. Activity continued to buzz around me, as the half-dozen FBI agents unloaded drawers, packed boxes and carried them away.

Agent Call sat on my right, while one of his colleagues took a seat to my left. The questioning began. When was the last time I had seen Todd? Was I aware that Todd was out of town? My answers were brief and simple. I knew very little about my ex-husband's comings and goings.

Then the questions took a turn I never could have predicted.

Agent Call looked into my eyes and gently asked, "Have you ever heard of NAMBLA?" He went on to explain that this was an acronym for North American Man/Boy Love Association.

A voice in my head began screaming "Man boy love? Man boy love? What does that mean?" Agent Call explained that Todd had been arrested an hour before in San Diego. He was there to catch a boat that was scheduled to take him and several traveling companions to Mexico, where they planned to engage in sex with minor boys.

Shock took over. I heard a distant, muffled moan escape my own mouth as I slumped over and began to cry. Despite our difficulties, I simply could not believe my ex-husband would do such a thing. I asked Agent Call if he was sure we were talking about the same man to whom I had been married for more than 10 years. He pulled out two pictures of Todd, confirming he was the man arrested earlier in the day.

My ex-husband, the father of my two precious children, was possibly a homosexual and a pedophile. How did I miss this?

Nausea filled my throat as the room began to spin. The agents spent the next hour reviewing the FBI's long-term sting operation. An FBI agent went undercover to attend at least two annual NAMBLA conventions, held in New York City in 2003 and Miami in 2004. The agent even assumed a leadership position on the organization's steering committee for its 2005 convention in San Diego. It was at the 2004 convention that the agent met Todd.

At a small café in Miami, Todd and several other NAMBLA members planned a four-day trip to Ensenada, Mexico, for the purpose of having sex with young boys. Just the day before today, on February 11, 2005, Todd followed through on those plans. He boarded an American Airlines flight from Dallas to San Diego. After landing in California, Todd met with NAMBLA members in the undercover agent's hotel room, where the group discussed the upcoming Mexico trip. They also reminisced about their past sexual encounters with young boys.

This very morning, Todd and his NAMBLA cohorts had traveled to a San Diego pier, where they were to catch a boat to Ensenada. The FBI swooped in and arrested them, followed by a search of Todd's business and house for additional evidence.

After my head was filled with the gruesome details, it was time to go. The agents helped me to my car and offered to accompany me home. I shakily refused and blindly drove the few blocks to my house, my children and a million questions about my life. And I pulled out my phone to start calling friends and family for help.

When I reached home, the kids came barreling down the stairs to greet me. Instead of seeing their typically enthusiastic mom, 10-year-old Austin and 8-year-old Alexa were met by my drawn face and swollen eyes. I explained that they would be spending the night with friends so that I could handle something that had happened with their dad. Despite the positive spin I tried to sell them, my children immediately sensed the gravity of the situation. They went upstairs to pack their bags and soon were whisked away for a night of pizza, sleeping bags and a respite from the reality that would soon come to roost in their lives.

My family gathered around me that afternoon and evening, and I told them every detail I could remember from my conversation with the FBI. I contacted my uncle, an attorney, fearing what ramifications the situation would have on our divorce decree regarding visitation and child support. As a mental fog set in, I was vaguely aware of phone conversations occurring between the attorneys and the FBI. Even now, when I try to recall details, the voices are muffled. I see myself roaming aimlessly throughout my home. I had lost my dreams, my organizational thinking skills, my ability to focus, and all feeling in my body. I was a walking, breathing shell of a human being. I felt like a puzzle on the verge of breaking into a thousand fragments.

As the details of the FBI's investigation took shape, I remained in denial. Surely this was a case of mistaken identity. How could I have known Todd for 12 years, yet missed this side of his personality? Suddenly it dawned on me that Todd's arrest could pop up in the newspaper or on TV. I wondered how much longer it would be before people outside the walls of my comfortable, peaceful Lakewood home would know what Dr. Todd Calvin had done.

Not a moment went by that my children weren't on my mind. I began to wonder whether Todd had molested my kids or their friends during an overnight stay. Even as my family and friends gathered to comfort me, this question repeated in my mind and became a constant source of anxiety.

Sunday, February 13, 2005

It was time to face my children.

The kids came in to the house solemnly, placed their bags in their rooms, and then sat with me in the den. The three of us curled up on our couch, with me in the middle. I told them something had happened involving their father. With a flat voice expressing little emotion, Austin asked if his father was dead. He assumed that his father had been killed in a crash in his private plane.

"No, honey," I gently explained. "Your dad is not dead. But he is in a lot of trouble."

I told these two small children that their father had been arrested. I didn't know all of the details yet, I said, but would know more very soon.

I listened to their questions and focused on answering what I could in simple terms. Like any good counselor, I told them the truth – but in small chunks they could manage and understand. My primary goal was to help ease their minds as much as possible.

At 8 and 10 years old, my children's questions were very basic. Was Dad in Dallas? Was he by himself? Did he go to San Diego in his airplane?

After I provided short and truthful responses to these simple questions, the conversation came to an abrupt end. Like most children in a crisis, my kids longed to resume normal activities. They had heard enough for right now.

The protective mom in me took my body and mind back from the professional counselor. I could now identify my purpose, both short-term and long-term. Somehow, I would find a way to make this okay for my children. We spent the rest of the afternoon hanging out and watching television. The children never mentioned the situation again.

In another effort to make the day as normal as possible, I took the kids to my parents' home for dinner, just as we had always done on Sunday evenings. After all, my children were looking to me to determine whether everything would be all right.

Then, the first hints of public humiliation surfaced. After we returned home from dinner, I received a phone call from our church pastor, Father John. He first inquired about me and the kids. This was followed, however, by a discussion I never could have anticipated. What was the best way, he asked, to handle this situation within the parish and school family? Our parish took part in a safe environment plan, which required rigorous screening of volunteers who had any contact with school or parish children. The plan outlined specific actions that must take place if a volunteer is arrested for a crime against a child.

Todd had been a regular volunteer at the school. But he had never been arrested for any prior criminal activity, so his background check had been clean. Father John explained that Todd would be banned from the school and church campus until this matter was resolved.

Father John then asked about my plans regarding the children and school. I had every intention of sending them to school the next day. After all, it was Valentine's Day, complete with class parties – always a highlight for my kids.

I began to question this decision. If the story broke in the local news, would my children be physically and emotionally safe at school? There were so many unknowns. Suddenly there was this sinister organization named NAMBLA in my world. FBI agents were swarming.

The pastor and I agreed to take things one day at a time. We would make decisions about sharing information with other school families when the time arose.

As I hung up the phone, my thoughts floated to the days and nights my children had spent visiting their father in his home. So many of their friends had been welcomed into that house to spend the night. Could he really be a pedophile? What if he had touched any of these children, including my own? How deep and entrenched was this betrayal in our life? Who was this man named Phillip Todd Calvin?

Monday, February 14, 2005

It was Valentine's Day.

I had mixed emotions about sending the children to school that morning, but the kids were determined to go. My parents offered to attend the Valentine's Day parties to keep an eye on them. After school, the kids would go home with my parents so that I could spend my day consulting with attorneys and the FBI, working to gain as much information as possible.

My instincts told me that this would hit the media at some point. This was big news, at least locally. Todd was a respected dentist with a million-dollar practice that had been featured on local television channels several times. His advertisements spanned the city, emphasizing his "family-oriented" practice and touting him as the dentist who "loves children."

That afternoon, Agent Call contacted me. The FBI in San Diego was holding a press conference about the sting operation and arrests, he said. During the press conference, the FBI would announce the names of those who were arrested.

I had so little time. Then everyone would know.

I didn't have long to wait. At 4:45 p.m., my television was tuned into *The Oprah Winfrey Show*. The local newscast broke in to report that the well-known "singing dentist" had been arrested by the FBI for interstate travel with the intent of engaging in sex with minor boys. There would be more details on the 5 p.m. news.

Now the world knew.

During the 5 p.m. and 6 p.m. newscasts that evening, every local television channel featured Todd's arrest as the first or second story. Each segment included pictures of Todd, some of which I had never even seen before. The reporters revealed the sketchy details of the sting operation and Todd's arrest, along with the arrests of two other men who were also members of NAMBLA.

My parents had successfully kept the children away from the television set during the news. We decided to go out to grab a quick bite to eat at the neighborhood Italian restaurant. I was concerned that we might run into an acquaintance who had heard the news, and I certainly didn't want the children learning the details from someone else. While we did see a few people we knew from church, it was obvious that none of them had seen the story yet. We ate quickly so we could return home. I needed to talk to the children.

Midway through the meal, I felt a strong inclination to call Todd's parents, Joe and Sue. Perhaps they did not know what was happening. They lived in a small Arkansas town, far from the events of the past few days. I stepped outside the restaurant and called my former father-in-law, Joe, who served as a county prosecutor in rural northeast Arkansas.

When he answered from his car, I asked him to pull over and listen carefully. I provided him the basic facts. And he simply did not believe me. While our divorce had been stressful on both of our families, Joe and I had maintained a positive and respectful relationship. His agitated response was startling to me. I assured him this was no joke and reiterated that I thought he should contact Todd's only brother and come to Dallas to speak with the FBI. We hung up. In tears, I went back into the restaurant and told my dad about my conversation. He took my phone, called Joe back and had a "father-to-father" conversation. Again, he encouraged Todd's father to come to Dallas.

Upon arriving home, I checked caller ID. My voicemail was overflowing. I ignored it, instead taking the kids to huddle on my king-sized bed.

As I prepared to shock my precious children, I realized something profoundly important. The conversation I was about to have with them was the very reason I had studied psychology, earned a master's degree and specialist certificate, and been trained to work with children facing crisis. All those years of studying, writing papers and going to lectures were culminating in this very moment. My children quietly watched me with a mixture of curiosity and confusion as my eyes welled up with tears.

I took a deep breath and gently told them why their father had been arrested. I used words like "inappropriate touching" to describe the accusation, and "sickness in his head" to help them understand how a significant adult in their life could have done these things.

At the tender age of 8, Alexa, my blue-eyed little girl, looked at me blankly, trying to take it all in. But my 10-year-old boy, Austin, had a startled look on his face. On the edge of puberty, his body was just beginning to change, and his curiosity about girls was in its early stages. At a time when he had all the natural questions about navigating relationships and his own physical development, how could this little man possibly grasp the concept that his father was a homosexual who preferred young boys right around his age?

Austin turned his head from me, but not before I glimpsed the redness around his eyes. He understood, and he was confused and hurting. I asked him what he was feeling. He quickly responded, "I don't care." He, too, was broken.

Alexa launched into a line of questioning fueled by curiosity. She asked, "What is he wearing?" and "What will he be eating?" I explained to the kids that this was a very big story here in Dallas because so many people knew their dad, so it was on all the news programs. My quiet little boy curled up next to me and simply stated, "So I guess everyone knows." I responded affirmatively. I assured both kids that our wonderful community of friends and family would love us, respect us and be supportive of us.

I explained to the children that they would not be going back to school for the rest of the week. The FBI, unbeknownst to the kids, needed to sit down with each child in a witness interview with a specially trained counselor. This would determine whether Austin and Alexa had any information pertinent to the case and, most importantly, whether they had been abused by their father. As I looked into their innocent eyes, I faced the question screaming in my head. Had Todd sexually abused my children? Just the thought of it, even to this day, makes me feel like someone has just thrown a hard punch to my gut.

An appointment with FBI agents and a counselor could not be scheduled at Dallas Children's Advocacy Center until Thursday. Until then, the children needed minimal contact with anyone who might discuss the details of the case or what was being reported in the media. I also wished to protect the kids from the initial reactions of schoolmates and neighbors, because I wasn't yet sure how people would respond to us. I assured the children that it would be a fun few days, during which they would visit with my parents and my sister and her husband. I think all they heard me say was "no school for the rest of the week."

By 9 p.m., my parents had taken the kids home with them. It was the beginning of another long night. The phone continued to ring, but I was not ready to answer. I slipped into pajamas and sat in front of my computer to read the several dozen emails that had come in just that evening. I read every email over and over again, as friends and acquaintances from church, school, the neighborhood and even my childhood years poured out their love and support for me and my children. Both phone calls and emails included offers of meals and prayers.

Tuesday, February 15, 2005

The children's school sent a letter to all school families assuring them that upon Todd's release, he was banned from the school premises. While we were not specifically named in the letter, our identities were impossible to hide. The morning began with both phone calls and knocks at the door by the media. Just about every local channel was interested in talking to me, in addition to *The Dallas Morning News* requesting a statement. I chose to make one statement to all of the media. I told them that the children and I were shocked and devastated, and I asked them to respect our privacy while we were going through the initial crisis.

The day was filled with meetings with the FBI and with my attorneys. I prepared a request for a restraining order to keep Todd away from me and the children, should he be granted bail. Todd's father and brother arrived. We had a conference call with Todd's court-appointed attorney to get as much information as we could. The day ended with Todd's brother speechless, and Todd's father angry and bewildered.

I operated in a fog as we carried on conversations about Todd, the man who had been my husband and was the father of my two children, yet now was pictured on the front page of *The Dallas Morning News*. I tried to focus on the tasks at hand and decisions that needed to be made. I cried countless tears, yet felt a detachment from everything going on around me. I wanted to lie down and die.

Wednesday, February 16, 2005

I was terrified by the thought of Todd being released on bail. I could not imagine anything worse than his walking through our community and reaching out to our children. During our divorce, he made it clear, both in his speech and in written letters, that he could easily and willingly commit suicide or leave the country in his private plane. Friends in other countries, he said, would help him avoid paying spousal and child support. If he had threatened these things during a relatively private divorce, what was he capable of when facing a very public trial? The stress of being caught and labeled a child predator would certainly push him past the edge of any reason he might have left.

Later that night, I finally hit rock bottom. I found myself curled on the marble floor surrounding my fireplace, sobbing. I could no longer hear family members having conversations around me. The bottom came when I acknowledged to myself on that very difficult evening that, despite my unconditional and deepest love for Austin and Alexa, I wanted to be dead. I prayed harder than I've ever prayed that night. Only by a miracle was I able to get up and dust myself off. There was no time for rock bottom. I had two children to raise.

Thursday, February 17, 2005

For almost six days, I had been haunted by a question. Did Todd molest my children?

It was time for their interviews at Dallas Children's Advocacy Center. Both together and individually, my children met with the FBI-appointed counselor, while agents watched from the other side of an observation mirror. The counselor's job was to determine what the children might have seen, what they knew and whether any harm had been done to them physically or emotionally during visits with their father.

It was the longest 90 minutes of my life. I sat like a statue in the waiting room, motionless except for my wringing hands.

When Austin and Alexa came out of their interviews,

ready for a snack of chips and drinks, the counselor and FBI agents debriefed me. While both children had probably seen some pornographic or "confusing" materials in their father's closet, the counselor was confident that neither child had been sexually molested. The FBI agents also felt there was no reason to believe that any of their friends had been molested.

The agents kindly reassured my kids that they were okay, they were normal and they had done nothing wrong. I took my children's little hands in mine as we walked down the steps from Dallas Children's Advocacy Center. While these sweet young children had lost a bit of their innocence and naiveté as a result of the last week's events, this joyous piece of news – that my children had not fallen prey to their father's urges – was my first sign of light at the end of a very dark tunnel.

It was time to begin a journey, just the three of us. We were a family, and we would be okay. I had no idea *how*, but I was their mother and fierce protector. From now on, it would be my job to help them navigate through life, despite this horrific set of circumstances. I was up for the challenge. In fact, it was the only thing that kept me moving forward, breathing in and out, taking one moment at a time. And so my journey began.

CHAPTER | 4

COMING OUT OF THE DARKNESS

Once my children were cared for and the initial shock wore off, I descended into darkness and pain. While the darkness was emotionally paralyzing, it was also blissfully quiet. I found comfort in the silence and numbness. Time passed in a blur, and the activities going on around me were white noise.

After about 10 days, however, the darkness parted ever so slightly to reveal a tiny bit of light. Unexpectedly, I found that light to be noisy, chaotic and painful.

For so many reasons, I could not bear to leave my home, and the media provided a small window to the world around me. Newspapers and television stations continued to run stories about Todd's arrest. The humiliation was almost unbearable as I tried to answer the questions of why and how. My children hesitantly returned to school, and a few friends stopped in here and there to check on us.

My old habits soon took over, shaking me out of my days-long reverie. I reverted to my Type-A self, who attacks a problem with a to-do list in one hand and a highlighter in the other.

I had a visit with my attorney. Todd's brother and father were included, and we all tried to determine what should be done with Todd's possessions. His home, car, boat and dental practice needed to be sold - quickly. Because I lived in Dallas and had connections that would help me sell these high-end items, Todd granted me his power of attorney for the time being.

Initially, I was repelled by the idea of selling this pedophile's belongings. But my practical self took over. I was told that the proceeds from the sales would be put into a brokerage account for my children, so that they would not suffer financially at the hands of a tragedy that had already confused them so much emotionally. I was doing this, I told myself, for my children.

Selling Todd's assets was a chaotic, draining task that provided more than a few shocks to my already overloaded system. His dental practice seemed like the easiest place to start. I entered its familiar doors and flipped on the lights. The building looked much the same as before – examination rooms with their reclining chairs, trays sitting ready to hold their army of dental tools. A few loose papers were scattered here and there, where FBI agents had thumbed through filing cabinets looking for evidence.

As I stepped into Todd's personal office, my heart began to race. The typically pristine room was in shambles. Locks on filing cabinets and desk drawers had been broken, and files had been rifled. I shuddered to imagine what evidence the FBI agents had hauled away, and I was grateful not to see it.

I planned to throw away Todd's personal papers and other documents unrelated to the dental practice. I flicked open a garbage bag and began working through the filing cabinets. As I flipped through file folders, a book caught my eye, and its subject matter shocked me. It gave pointers on living a gay lifestyle. As I pulled out item after item, I uncovered blatant proof of my husband's decade-long secret life. NAMBLA newsletters. A used condom. A newsletter from the Gay Pilots Association. More books about homosexuality.

The truth was in my hands. Todd didn't have feelings for women in general, much less me. And he wasn't just a gay man who had married for convenience or friendship. He was a monster who preyed on children. Like never before, I saw that our entire marriage had been an act on Todd's part. It was orchestrated for his benefit, to create the image of a successful businessman the community could trust.

I pulled two photos from a file folder. Smiling back at me from one was a young adolescent male, one of Todd's favorite patients. The other photo shook me to my core. It showed a group of preteen boys, clad in swimsuits and grinning into the camera. These friends were palling around at a birthday party. I searched the faces of the boys and found my son and his buddies. I had seen this picture before, as I lovingly thumbed through memories in a scrapbook. I had admired my sweet son and his cute young friends, enjoying their childhood. No more. Now, this photo represented sickness. My deviant ex-husband had used this photo for his sexual fantasies. I could never see innocent family photos the same way again. Betrayal.

I waded through the rest of the office, growing numb to what I found. At last, it was finished. I locked up and went home to recuperate.

Next, I had to face Todd's house. My father offered to help, but I declined. This was something I had to do alone. My parents already had suffered so much through this ordeal, and I could not subject my dad to what I knew was probably lurking within those four walls.

A few days later, I steeled my resolve and walked into Todd's large house, garbage bags in hand. I had to empty the home of personal items, plus inventory the furniture and other saleable items. Even after my horrifying experience in Todd's office, I was not prepared for what I found. In the study was a receipt for a pornographic video of pre-pubescent boys. A kitchen cabinet overflowed with catalogs and magazines featuring nude men. These pictures could be easily found by anyone – even visiting children.

I remembered what the FBI agents had said. Predators groom their victims by showing them pornography. As I threw the mounds of filth into garbage bags, I howled in rage and pain, the tears streaming down my face. How long had this gone on? And was Todd working his way up to victimizing my son or his friends?

I dragged the trash to my car, took it home and burned it.

Slowly and methodically, I worked my way through the sale of Todd's possessions. As I attacked task after task, I was faced with a new challenge. It started with a call from San Diego.

"Your husband has requested bail," said a representative from the U.S. attorney's office. "I'm working on a recommendation to the judge. Since you're Dr. Calvin's ex-wife and have custody of his children, your opinions are important."

My heart filled with fear. Could Todd get out on bail, leaving him free to try and see the kids?

I answered the attorney's questions clearly and honestly. Was Todd a danger to himself or others? Yes. Was Todd a flight risk? Yes. I gave numerous examples showing why Todd should not be released from custody.

Suddenly, I remembered the letter Todd had written during our divorce, when he threatened to flee the country simply to avoid paying support. It provided further evidence that was vital to the prosecution's recommendation.

Twice, Todd attempted to be released on bail. Twice, he was denied. Because I had spoken to the prosecuting attorneys, Todd placed the blame squarely on me. He wrote a letter to his parents claiming that I had done everything possible to keep him in jail, as though his circumstances were my fault, rather than his own. Unfortunately, from that moment, my former in-laws turned their backs on me and their grandchildren.

The legal process was proceeding. I had taken inventory of Todd's possessions. Now, it was time to take inventory of myself. The counselor needed some counseling.

* * *

I began spending emotional sessions with John, an amazing therapist who helped me work through the whirlwind of recent events. No matter how much information I revealed about my marriage or how many tears I cried, John simply shook his head.

"You're in denial," he said. "You think you can fool me, just because of your background in psychology?"

"I just want to talk it out and get better," I argued. "When am I going to feel better? When will I be healed?"

John sighed. "Not everything fits into a neat timeline," he said. "First, you have to face up to the truth."

I was stymied. I couldn't understand what had happened to my life, my husband and my safe little world. How could I find any overarching truth? Even more disturbing to me, I lost the power to dream – both by day and by night.

Prior to my ex-husband's arrest, I had always been a

dreamer. During daylight hours, I was spirited and filled with ideas. I would imagine myself in the future, living in a vast array of exciting scenarios. As I slept, my mind was filled with enchanted dreams that were life-size and in color, full of bright scenes and action-packed adventure. From childhood, I had entertained my friends and family by recounting the exciting stories that filled my sleep.

Now, my dreams had evaporated. There was no color and no imagination. My nighttime dreams had vanished, and my daylight dreams were gone. How could I possibly imagine a future? After all, everything I had known to be truth was, in reality, a lie. Because I might find the truth in my dreams, they had become too dangerous for my psyche to handle. In an instinctive act of self-protection, my brain blocked my dreams from my consciousness.

I remained emotionally trapped. Then, one session with John became a turning point.

"For just a few minutes, I want you to stop being the victim," John said. "Be a professional, an associate psychologist, just like you were trained and licensed to be."

"Okay," I said. "Now what? You want me to diagnose myself?"

"No," he said, with a twinkle in his eye. "I want you to be completely objective. And I want you to diagnose Todd Calvin."

In all our years of marriage, it had never occurred to me. I had the tools at my fingertips to explain this man with whom I had lived, made children and divorced. I spent a few moments of meditative silence and then, slowly, began listing symptoms.

A short time later, I had diagnosed Todd as narcissistic, a pathological liar and a sociopath. No wonder I felt so emotionally battered after 10 years of marriage to this man, I thought.

"You cannot control Todd's actions," John said. "You couldn't control them during your marriage, and you can't control them now. But you can understand the facts. He is what he is. And now, you can see that more clearly than ever before."

The floodgates opened. My defenses were broken. At last, I understood. And I could accept what was the truth. That flicker of light at the end of the tunnel became much brighter. Despite my fear, I was ready to move toward that light.

Betrayal recovery could begin.

SECTION 2

SPOTTING THE PREDATOR NEXT DOOR

You gain strength, courage and confidence by every experience in which you really stop to look fear in the face. You are able to say to yourself, 'I have lived through this horror. I can take the next thing that comes along.' You must do the thing you think you cannot do.

—Eleanor Roosevelt

CHAPTER | 5

WHAT MAKES A PREDATOR?

My ex-husband was in jail. I had witnessed his erratic behavior during a decade of marriage. I had even dug through piles of pornography hidden in his home. Yet I still had a hard time digesting the idea that Todd was a predator.

To fulfill my desperate need to understand, I embarked on a frenzy of research. I started with the astonishing documents from Todd's court case. The case wound its way through a cast of disturbing characters, including pedophiles and NAMBLA members.

As I delved into deeper research, I discovered that the characteristics of child predators are amazingly consistent. As I learned more about these manipulative monsters, I realized that simply talking to my kids about stranger-danger was not enough to keep them out of harm's way. More difficult was acknowledging that Todd displayed virtually all of the characteristics of a pedophile. In our family's little world, I had explained away these danger signs. In some cases, I even considered them beneficial to our relationship. I had compartmentalized myself into a wife and discarded my psychological counseling skills. Had I been able to view him more objectively through the lens of a psychologist, I might have seen the red flags for what they were.

Many predators are sociopaths - people born without empathy. This enables them to abuse others without feeling their

victims' pain. Sociopaths never see the world the way "normal" people do, nor do they fully grasp the painful consequences of their actions. They fake emotions, but never actually feel them.
Following are the common characteristics of child predators, as well as related insights from my own experiences.

Child predators sometimes struggle privately with adult intimacy. Yet they also tend to be likeable, well-respected members of the community.

Most adults do not talk openly about their physical intimacy with other adults, whether in previous or current relationships. Child predators, however, take this typical behavior to extremes. Many child predators struggle with both the physical and emotional aspects of intimate adult relationships. This may be the result of their own victimization during childhood. Or, it may simply come from the fact that close relationships require trust, as well as knowing the other adult at a deeper level. Such intimacy becomes a threat, making it difficult for predators to maintain their secrecy. If they become physically or emotionally close with other adults, child predators fear they could be discovered and derailed. In the community at large, however, predators create a convincing front, making it appear as though they are involved in the kind of productive relationships that create a positive, upstanding image.

When we were dating, I peppered Todd with typical questions about past girlfriends. He told me about his last relationship with a single mother who had young children. Todd went into lengthy detail describing the kids. He would babysit them on occasion, he said, and he loved to take them places. For all of his conversation about those children, Todd said precious little about their mother.

Our own dating scenario offered subtle clues. At age 33, Todd made no attempt to kiss me goodnight until our third date. Even then, I subtly initiated the peck.

Three months later, we had not progressed much further. Todd seemed to enjoy my company and spending time together, but he stopped short of pursuing a physical relationship. Because I had endured several tough relationships and breakups, I appreciated Todd's attitude and considered it refreshingly old-fashioned and respectful - at least that is what I told myself. On the other hand, I wouldn't have minded if he had made a few advances. After all, I could always reject them.

At the close of one date, we stopped off at Todd's house after dinner. I was feeling the effects of a little too much wine and blurted out, "Are you gay?" Todd first looked stunned, but then began to laugh. He asked, "What makes you think that?" He then smoothly claimed that he was merely showing his respect for me. Of course, Todd said, he found me attractive. I ignored my intuition, which had prompted me to ask a seemingly inappropriate question at a time my guard was down.

Shortly after we married, I expected our physical relationship to peak. Instead, I was surprised that it remained sparse and mechanical - unless we were trying to conceive. As the years went by, Todd deflected my attempts to initiate sex by insulting me. He called me unattractive. When I was pregnant, he claimed that my bump was a turn-off. After I gave birth to two children, he said sex was no longer enjoyable. Todd knew how to hit me in the most vulnerable area by attacking my weight. These attacks made me cower and withdraw from physical contact.

Todd seemed to avoid friendships. He preferred spending time on his own. I explained that away by citing the hours upon hours he spent building a dental practice. At the time, I enjoyed socializing with friends, as well as members of our church and parents at our children's school. This was daunting for Todd, who would explain that he was just not as comfortable with people as I was. Thinking he had a shy nature, I did not argue and often went to events solo. Todd's isolation, however, went beyond avoidance of my friends. He never seemed to forge close friendships with adults in any arena, professionally, as a pilot or elsewhere.

At the same time, he could blather on for endless minutes and hours about the children he had met, as well as their individual interests. Back then, this intense focus on young people seemed charming and endearing. Today, with my knowledge of Todd's proclivities, the memory sickens me.

Child predators may have been abused as children.

Many individuals who prey upon and abuse children were themselves victims of abuse. As child victims, these eventual predators become detached and develop a dysfunctional understanding of adult/child relationships, intimacy and sex. It must be pointed out, however, that some child predators were not abused as children. Sometimes, they came from a dysfunctional family life or experienced dysfunctional family relationships that, while not considered "abusive," were emotionally powerful enough to feed the predator's need to control and abuse. And other predators were simply born that way.

Todd maintained a love/hate relationship with his parents and brother. When asked about them, he could easily reel off an extensive list of irritations. We traded visits with them during the holidays. During these times, Todd appeared annoyed by his mother.

He seemed to enjoy bashing his father to anyone who would listen. Growing up, Todd was not an athlete or a typically mischievous boy. Because of this, he felt ignored and picked on by his father, who instead spent time playing ball or going on outings with Todd's brother. Todd stayed home with his mother, who supposedly sheltered him because he had asthma. As an adult, Todd's brother kept his distance. He worked overseas for several years and rarely spoke with Todd, even after moving back to the United States.

Of course, none of this constitutes abuse. Yet, in hindsight, it points to a degree of dysfunction in the family.

Keep in mind that most victims of child abuse do not grow up to be abusers themselves. They are not doomed to repeat the cycle. There is no direct cause-and-effect that can be traced from abuse to abuser, nor from dysfunctional family to abuser.

Those who do grow up to oppress others are responsible for their own behaviors, no matter what they may have endured as children.

Child predators seek out children who are shy, vulnerable or easily manipulated.

Child predators live a secret life – a life of fantasies. They look to real life to provide the characters for those fantasies, and they prefer children who are the easiest to lure into their twisted world. The typical child predator does not want to conquer a child who presents a challenge by avoiding contact or fighting back. Rather, he seeks out a child in need: the lonely child in a single-parent household, the child who struggles socially and just wants to be accepted, or the child struggling with his own sexual identity and feeling alone in a crowded world, just to name a few examples. In addition, child predators look for children who are neglected, because the parents may not be present or willing to defend their kids.

During our courtship, Todd talked about mentoring young boys during his time as a youth minister or camp counselor. He could recount minute details of his relationship with each boy and would become animated and emotional when speaking about them. Once upon a time, I found these tales so endearing. Now, they are sickening.

The story of one boy, Jeremy, is still etched in my brain. Like most of the young boys Todd "helped," Jeremy was 12 or 13 and from a broken family. He had been physically abused by his father and now was living with his mother, who was often absent trying to make a living. Jeremy felt comfortable enough in his friendship with Todd to share all his sadness and darkness, and Todd was there to comfort him. I vividly remember Todd recounting the day he learned Jeremy had committed suicide. The emotions were raw, even though many years had passed. Now I wonder if that young boy took his own life to avoid what might have transpired between him and Todd Calvin.

Child predators generally need to control or have power over others.

As mentioned earlier, many child predators were victimized as children. This put them in a powerless position where they were controlled by physical abuse, emotional torment and the lies of their abuser. Then, later in life, child predators transform their prior position of weakness into a need for control. That need is not necessarily limited to their abuse victims. Oftentimes, child predators also display controlling behaviors and a need for dominance in marriage, at work and in other relationships. Yet at the same time, the predator maintains a charismatic and likeable personality in the public eye.

When Todd was building his dental practice, he often admitted that he felt out of control. Yet in his volunteer positions with children, Todd was comfortable. He was the respected adult who was fun, trusted by kids and adults alike, and who "understood" children. Todd put a premium on discipline, but struggled with choosing his battles. He longed to be proved right, in an effort to establish dominance over the situation. As a result, at home he could argue about an insignificant issue for days. He would even take surveys of his staff and patients on silly topics, like whether his socks matched his pants. Then, he believed, he could come home and declare himself victor in an argument I never made. It was all a sick game to him, and one he was determined to win.

Child predators typically have a low self-esteem.

In many cases, child predators were abused physically or victimized emotionally in an unhealthy, dysfunctional environment during childhood. Some may abhor their sexual desire for a child and know that these feelings are unnatural and unacceptable in our society. As a result, they are plagued by low self-esteem, leading to feelings of inferiority with most other adults or strong, confident children. The predator's overwhelming need to be loved and accepted can lead to a warped misinterpretation of children's innocent actions as "invitations to touch." The child predator can psychologically misconstrue his abusive "affections" toward a child by rationalizing that the child wants or deserves these "affections."

Admittedly, Todd's low self-esteem was an attraction when we met. I had my own self-esteem issues, especially when it came to men and relationships. As a result, I relished the idea of someone needing me to give them a boost of self-assurance. I loved that this educated, nice-looking man wanted my help. We would even discuss our respective childhood self-esteem issues, from his lack of masculinity to my weight.

Until the last few years of our marriage, I failed to understand that Todd's low self-esteem actually resulted in emotional abuse. He did not like who he was. And if he didn't like himself, he sure wasn't going to live with someone who liked herself. As we neared divorce, he used words like "fat" and "a nothing" to describe what he saw when he looked at me. He told me to "enjoy your friendships with your rich friends while you can, because once we divorce and you are poor, they will want nothing to do with you." By then, I was far more confident in how I looked, how I parented, my friendships and my professional life, so his words could no longer hurt me.

Child predators prefer the company of children and will often seek out occupations and volunteer opportunities to feed this need.

Plain and simple, the child predator has surging desires to look at, talk to, touch and molest children. Regardless of how he might rationalize these needs or behaviors, he puts himself in scenarios that lead to interaction with children. Read any news story detailing a child-abuse case. In almost every situation, the predator placed himself in a situation filled with children: parks, ball fields, schools, church youth groups, camps, toy stores, and a host of professional industries that specialize in serving children. The child predator might be outstanding at his calling as minister, teacher, pediatric physician or camp counselor. Nonetheless, he chose that profession to indulge his need to engage with children.

I thought Todd was such an incredible gift. Imagine, as a young woman, finding an attractive, educated guy who not only wants to build a life with you, but also loves kids and cannot wait to be a parent. Plus, he looks forward to participating in all of your volunteer efforts – at least those that relate to children.

Todd had a dream resume: counselor with a prestigious Texas summer camp for kids, youth leader for his church's youth group and mentor to neighborhood kids who needed a sympathetic ear. Later in our marriage, Todd used his private-pilot license to take children up in his plane as part of a "Young Eagles" program. He volunteered to fly children to hospitals in other cities for necessary medical treatments. He volunteered at the annual carnival at our children's school, willingly working hours on end. At work, he even created marketing pieces that touted "we love children." The community – especially the kids – respected and liked Todd, from all outward appearances. In reality, he undertook all of these volunteer opportunities to feed his need for contact with pre-pubescent boys.

When I uncovered and understood these characteristics, it

answered only a few of my many questions about Todd Calvin as a child predator. Then, I began to expand my definition of a predator. After all, to my family, Todd was also a perpetrator of betrayal. He preyed on me, our children and our entire community, inflicting collateral damage on all of us.

What were the characteristics of an emotionally abusive mate who led a double life, compartmentalized his relationships to protect his secret, and betrayed hundreds of people he claimed as family and friends?

I was astonished to realize that perpetrators of other kinds of betrayals display characteristics similar to those of a child predator.

They:

- have difficulty establishing close relationships

- have low self-esteem

- need to control situations and people

- display neediness

- are perceived as loving, lovable and charismatic

I experienced every one of these characteristics in Todd. Yet they were subtle compared to his other, more positive character traits: involved in his community, a hard-working and successful dentist, well-liked by his patients, upper-middle class and an adoring parent.

In hindsight, I wail, "How did I miss this?" But the rational, professional side of me knows that most people with this set of characteristics are not predators. They might be addicts, neurotics or people-pleasers. Unfortunately, there is no easy way to spot a predator in the crowd – especially because most people are not actively looking for them.

Chapter | 6

Recognizing the Danger Signs

After my description of a predator in Chapter 5, as well as my analysis of Todd, it all seems so clear. How could I have not known that my husband was a predator?

The answer to this question has haunted me for years. "Predator" is a strong word. It evokes the image of a dark, shady brute – perhaps an uneducated, low-class bully. Sure, caricatures like these do exist in real life. But they are easy to spot, because they stand out with their stark, threatening profiles. More difficult to discern are the subtle predators, who convince others that they are harmless or even beneficial.

We tell our children about stranger-danger. We show them educational programming that portrays predators as people who are monstrous, unattractive and evil. We suggest that these "bad" people might act strangely and trigger a red flag. We warn kids away from dangerous places at particular times.

Yet we fail to address reality. We don't explain – or even understand – that predators are masters of disguise. They don't look like hideous monsters who stand out from the crowd. Instead, they are someone's grandpa, soccer coach or other trusted adult.

•

Predators come in all shapes, sizes, socioeconomic status, genders and races:

- a man seeking cover so he can lead a double life, whether as an adulterer, pedophile or other predator

- the kind voice on the other end of the phone, trying to convince an elderly victim to send money for the promise of a prize

- a teacher, coach or other trusted adult who preys upon children

- a serial philanderer who lures a man into her trap with charisma and charm, only to dump him after taking his money and ability to trust

- a perpetrator of domestic violence who seeks out victims to live with, marry, control and dominate

- a rapist who follows his victims and waits for the perfect scenario to physically control and hurt them

- a con artist who hides behind the façade of a charitable cause to collect money from giving individuals, only to steal it for her own purposes

Any of us can be fooled. But when we understand some of the most basic characteristics of predators, and prioritize those facts above less important concepts such as status or reputation, we are empowered to make better personal choices. These choices, in turn, empower our children to remain free from predators.

That's why looking for signs of predatory behavior cannot be the primary focus. Rather, we must carefully understand and control our personal reactions to subtle red flags that will protect us and the ones we love. No longer can we trust others automatically. We must listen to our instincts. And, above all else, we must be willing to recognize and confront evil.

Imagine that you meet the "boy next door." He's an

accomplished minister, a caring coach, an inspiring teacher or a stellar neighbor. He may be talented and well-respected, on the job or in the neighborhood. Should these factors make you trust him automatically? Definitely not.

For a while, keep your guard up. Take your time getting to know the person. Ask questions, and listen to the answers with both your head and your heart. Does he ever make you uncomfortable? If so, never be afraid to walk away – whatever the expense.

Society has trained us to be concerned about appearances and the opinions of others beyond all else. I urge you to turn this notion on its head. Your gut reaction should take precedence. It has more credibility than appearances ever could.

Like the majority of predators today, our predator was the "boy next door." He was highly educated, upper-middle class, a husband and father, well-respected in the community, likable and fun, a model citizen and a good neighbor.

Our predator was a leader in the community and financially prosperous. He had a million-dollar dental practice, a home in an upscale neighborhood, a sailboat and his own private plane.

To a vulnerable young girl desperate for happiness, our predator looked just like Prince Charming. He was a master of lies, and I was eager to be in a relationship. My gut sent me a sign or two, but I ignored them, instead focusing on his positive attributes.

Our predator sought me out as cover for his double life. He needed a façade to hide his urges and needs. At some point, he may have even rationalized our model life, hoping it would help him resist temptations.

After I acknowledged that Todd was not only a predator of children, but also a predator of me, an interesting question arose. Did the true betrayal of my family occur the day Todd was arrested? Or did it take place years before, when I met, married and trusted him?

Were there subtle danger signs? Were there red flags that I simply ignored during our marriage or, even more importantly, during our courtship?

There are many predatory characteristics that may or may not exist in every predator. Overwhelmingly, predators have a need to control you, their environment, and their victims. If you are with someone who needs to control and dominate, you are potentially in danger.

They may:

- be vague in responses about previous relationships

- prefer to spend time alone

- want to isolate you from friends and family

- lose their temper easily

- act violently

- be intrusive with your personal space, including your mobile phone, home, mail or e-mail

- appear self-centered

- have the need to always be "right"

- offer a disturbing view of social or humanitarian issues

- rush the relationship

These signs may trigger a negative gut instinct. If that happens, please walk away – immediately.

On the flip side, predators can trigger danger signs that exist within ourselves – in our own personalities, emotions and actions. Do you have certain behaviors that, when you step outside of yourself, you can observe objectively and acknowledge might guide the choices you make in relationships? Here are some things to look for in your own behaviors and attitudes.

Avoid these to reduce your chances of becoming a victim:

- low self- esteem

- lack of personal-space boundaries

- fear of asking in-depth questions

- too much concern about the opinions of others

- positive outlook becoming negative

- a view that your happiness relies on a particular relationship

- moving the relationship to the next level too quickly

- ignoring your gut instinct to walk away

Keep in mind that the observations of your most trusted friends and relatives can provide great insight into your relationships. You can learn a great deal by soliciting honest feedback from friends and family. They know your personal blind spots and can detect your negative patterns – before you do.

Above all, ask questions, take relationships slowly and go with your gut. Never be afraid to walk away.

CHAPTER | 7

PEDOPHILES, THE ULTIMATE PREDATORS

Every 11 seconds, a child is abused. One out of four girls and one out of six boys will be sexually abused before their 18th birthdays. In more than 90 percent of child abuse cases, children are not abused by strangers.

Just as there is no clear description of a child predator, there is no secret weapon against them. Of course, age-appropriate communication with children helps build a shield of protection around them. Before you can explain child predators to your children, it helps to have a more in-depth understanding of these monsters.

In a behavioral analysis of the child predator, "pedophile" is a diagnostic term given to an individual who has a sexual preference for children. Pedophilia is defined by the American Psychiatric Association's *Diagnostic and Statistical Manual* as "recurrent, intense, sexually arousing fantasies, sexual urges or behaviors involving sexual activity with a pre-pubescent child." That's it. No long list of physical descriptors or obvious danger signs.

Not all pedophiles actually act upon their sexual urges and fantasies. This makes it even harder to spot the predators. Law enforcement regularly refers to various degrees of pedophilia, which many place on a sort of continuum. At one end are those who feed their urges visually – viewing child pornography or watching children at the neighborhood playground. A little further along are pedophiles who work or volunteer in jobs that allow them easy access to children, yet do not act on their urges physically. Then come pedophiles who produce and distribute child pornography, followed by those who act upon their fantasies by having sex with minor children. Finally, some pedophiles become involved in organizations whose members meet and conspire to have sex with children.

Yes, that information is repulsive to contemplate. But remember, pedophiles can look perfectly normal from the outside. They might be homosexual, heterosexual or bisexual. The majority of the time, pedophiles are men with no criminal record. Oftentimes, these men are married and use their wives as façades to mask their true urges and preferences.

In most cases, pedophiles:

- are popular and well-liked by children

- prefer the company of children

- are considered trustworthy and respectable members of the community

- groom children with quality time, toys, video games, money or other gifts

- groom adults in the child's life by offering to babysit, provide free lessons or tutoring, all while gaining trust

- single out children who appear emotionally fragile or in need of attention

- date or marry women with children who are the ages of their preferred victims

- introduce physical contact with the child gradually, usually through trust and being the child's friend

Again, the question arises: How can we keep children safe?

One-on-one communication with your kids

- Worry more about your children's safety than about the possibility of scaring them with the information.

- With young children, talk about "private parts" using the proper anatomical names. Describe off-limits areas as "all the places your bathing suit covers." Tell them that nobody should touch them in these areas except a doctor, and that should happen only with a parent present.

- At all ages, discuss physical boundaries with children. Try this exercise. Walk outside and have your child stand on the driveway. Using chalk, draw three concentric circles around him or her. Explain that these are the circles of comfort. The outside circle is for strangers. The middle circle includes friends, schoolmates, teammates and close family members. The inner circle – or personal circle – is always within their own control. Explain to your child that he decides who comes into that circle – close enough for a hug – and who does not. This discussion will empower your child to control what goes on in his or personal circle.

- For teens and tweens, help them look beyond the opinions of others. Give them permission to feel uncomfortable in any situation, extract themselves by any means possible, and talk to you without being second-guessed or presumed guilty.

Youth sports

- Attend your child's practices.

- Make sure the sports organization runs background checks on coaches.

- If your child's team travels, there should be other adults who supervise off-site trips. Your child should never be alone with the coach during team sleepovers or trips.

- Be cautious of any coach who shows a particular interest in your child, plays favorites, makes promises of developing your child as a champion player, or sets private meetings or events with your child.

Youth camps

- Make sure background checks are done on all camp counselors.

- Make sure your child is never alone with a camp counselor.

- Encourage your child to travel in groups, whether he or she is engaging in recreational activities or going for a short walk to the restroom.

School

- Keep an eye out for teachers who want to spend additional, one-on-one time with your child, either before or after school.

- Instruct your child to immediately leave a restroom facility where he or she is alone with one adult.

- Ask the school administrator or technology coordinator about the school computer Internet safety policies and procedures.

Home

- When your child talks about a particular coach, teacher or other adult, listen. If he or she expresses discomfort with the adult in charge or suddenly wants to quit the sport or activity, consider it a warning sign. Talk these feelings through with your child.

- Encourage your child to "go with his gut" in any uncomfortable situation.

- Don't dismiss your child's discomfort with a trusted adult without probing further and keeping the lines of communication open. Remember, it is those trusted, community-valued adults who are so often the predators next door.

In the community

Predators do exist, right in your own community. It is idealistic to believe that all predators are easy to spot, catch and punish. It is time for us, as individuals and as a community, to move our focus away from the predator and onto ourselves and our families.

We must look inside ourselves first and take control of our decision-making processes when building relationships with others. This includes taking responsibility for our own strengths and weaknesses, knowing the danger signs of potentially damaging relationships, and having the courage to talk about these things. Even better, we can become leaders in taking action throughout our communities. None of these actions will completely eliminate the threat of predators in our lives or the lives of our children. But they will reduce our risk of falling victim.

- Encourage your child's school to re-direct its "stranger-danger" message. At the age-appropriate level, kids should be told about the reality that a person who wants to harm them might very well be someone they know. Then, include tips to kids on how they can keep themselves safe by making good decisions.

- Include tips on keeping kids safe (available on a host of web sites included in this book's appendices) in your homeowners' association newsletter or other neighborhood communications.

- Seek out guest speakers for your neighborhood churches and schools to talk to parents, grandparents and anyone who works with children. Talking about this vital topic is half the battle.

- Send an email blast to everyone in your address book, providing information on how to keep children safe from predators. Link to an online video about preventing child abuse. Your local Children's Advocacy Center can probably help with this task.

- Create a neighborhood Crimes Against Children Watch Group that serves as the eyes and ears of neighborhood parents, looking out for each other's children or communicating the presence of a registered sex offender living in your community.

Online

In today's world, the Internet makes devious behavior even easier for many pedophiles, who take their fantasies further than most people can even imagine. Pedophiles can gather online, providing literature for other pedophiles on how to seduce children. Pedophiles can even join sex rings over the Internet through groups such as NAMBLA, which supports the normalization and legalization of pedophilia.

In Internet forums and chat rooms, pedophiles assure fellow child predators that their behaviors are normal and teach them to rationalize their behaviors. They lure innocent children into their traps, taking and sharing pictures and videos using digital cameras and webcams. They hope this grooming will culminate in face-to-face meetings for sex – or worse. With this in mind:

- Keep your computer in a family room or a space that is easily accessed by all family members.

- When your child is online, walk in unexpectedly from time to time. Your child will understand the limitations of privacy when it comes to his or her online behaviors

- Know your own computer. With kids so technologically advanced, it is incumbent upon parents to perform due diligence. Know how to find your child's web-browsing history and chat logs.

- Forbid your children to erase their history files.

- Do not allow webcams.

- Instruct your child, tween and teen to never give out his or her real name or any identifying information on the Internet. Remind them that the person they are talking to might not be who they say they are. Make sure their screen name does not divulge anything that identifies them.

- Know their passwords.

- Use an ISP that allows you to block your child from accessing certain areas or sites.

- Instruct your child to never arrange a face-to-face meeting with someone he or she has met on the Internet.

- If your child receives an image or message that is uncomfortable, harassing or possibly pornographic, instruct the child to tell you, without fear of consequences.

    Let me share a personal story, direct from a home that has been affected by a child predator. My daughter Alexa enjoyed spending time in a Mom-approved chat room with her school friends. The girls were messaging about schoolwork, boys and other typically girl-subjects when a new friend named Annie appeared.

As I passed by the computer, I checked Alexa's buddy list and saw the unfamiliar name.

"Who is Annie?" I asked conversationally, so as not to pique my daughter's suspicion or put her on the defensive.

"She goes to another school. I'm not sure which one," Alexa said casually. "She's 12, just like me, and she knows some of the other girls I chat with."

I asked to see the history of Annie's instant messages. My suspicions immediately rose. Annie referred to the girls in the chat room only by their screen names. Clearly, this "girl" was not anybody's personal friend. Annie's notes to my daughter were verbally aggressive, including name-calling and snide innuendo.

Then, I saw the punch line. Annie's last message to my daughter requested a one-on-one chat the next day between 9 and 11 in the morning. And the next day was a school day.

"Honey, where will you be tomorrow from 9 until 11?" I asked gently.

"In school, of course," she replied innocently.

"Sweetheart, I don't believe Annie is who you think she is," I said. "Annie is probably an older man who wants to talk to you alone, so he can find out more about you. Then, he would try to convince you to meet him in person. That way, he could hurt you."

"Mom, how could you possibly know that?" she objected.

"I don't know it for a fact," I said. "But the warning signs are there, and my gut reaction is to get away from Annie. In this house, we don't ignore warning signs or gut feelings."

"Annie does seem a little strange," Alexa agreed.

We erased "Annie" from my daughter's buddy list and blocked any further access.

Most kids who get into bad situations as a result of Internet chat are just like my daughter. They are good children who need someone to talk with them, set solid ground rules and empower them. Armed with the truth, these kids are no longer viable victims, and the predator moves on.

But what about those who already have been victimized by a predator, either directly or through betrayal of their trust? How can they become whole again to live, love and trust?

SECTION 3

RECOVERING FROM BETRAYAL

Character cannot be developed in ease and quiet. Only through experiences of trial and suffering can the soul be strengthened, vision cleared, ambition inspired and success achieved.

-Helen Keller

CHAPTER | 8

SHATTERED...BUT PICKING UP THE PIECES

The day I first learned of my ex-husband's betrayal, my body went into physical shock. This common response is the body's way of handling heavy burdens, allowing victims time to calm themselves before they react to difficult or stressful situations. But 24 hours later, the physical signs of shock were gone. I was left in mental anguish and turmoil. And I was in full-blown crisis.

Once betrayal becomes obvious, how can its victims pick up the pieces and resume a normal life? At the time, I had no answers to this complex question. Both professionally and as the busy mom of two children in a single-parent household, I had always been pegged as a super-organized, Type-A personality. My reputation centered on clear thinking and solid decision-making. But where was the clarity now?

I vividly remember sitting in our church and gazing at the 60-year-old stained-glass windows. Like a thunderbolt, an idea struck my mind. That window was me. I was a beautiful stained-glass window, now shattered into millions of tiny pieces. But I was left with no guide for re-creating the original work of art. Where should I begin picking up the pieces, much less assembling them into something resembling a life?

Betrayal can come at any age and in any package: a spouse or loved one, a friend, our own body, or even a feeling of betrayal by God. In the months after my ex-husband's arrest, I was amazed and inspired by the stories others shared with me. A friend confided that her childhood years were marred by an abusive uncle, yet she had never told anyone about her pain. A woman shared that her husband had cheated with three different women in the course of a year. A beautiful and kind stranger in the airplane seat next to me felt betrayed by God when she was diagnosed with stage-four cancer while tending to her son severely injured in Iraq. In each case, someone these people loved had broken their trust and left them shattered.

As a result of these betrayals, we all felt as though trapped in quicksand and sinking fast. Even more disturbing, we wondered whether we would ever pull ourselves out and walk away.

I tried to back away and view our situations through a professional lens. Could this simply be one of the stages of grief, which run the emotional gamut from denial and anger to bargaining, depression and eventual acceptance? No, I concluded, these emotions went far deeper than a typical grief reaction. Plus, while I was willing to experience the denial and depression stages, I refused to become angry. If I experienced and expressed anger, I believed Todd would somehow win.

Despite my pain and uncertainty, I longed to pull out of the emotional quicksand. My personal stained-glass window had to be soldered back together, no matter how much time and pain was required. I clung desperately to the belief that, once I was no longer shattered, my stained-glass window would be more beautiful than ever. Sure, the cracks and crazing would be visible. But light would shine in and fill every room with joy.

I had to find a starting place and devise a path to healing. Who would help me? How would I find them? What should I do?

My struggle culminated in Journey Steps, a series of exercises and strategies to aid in betrayal recovery. As I continue to share my story with you, I will explain the Journey Steps. By weaving them into my personal history, I hope to better illustrate how victims of betrayal can heal.

Journey Step 1: Take one moment at a time

Rather than taking on my usual bull-by-the-horns persona,

I turned inward. I began to cocoon myself, both physically and mentally. Life became white noise and lost its meaning. Despite the friends and family who gathered close to comfort me, I landed in my darkest place. I couldn't concentrate. I couldn't sleep. Always a planner in the past, I now panicked when I tried to envision the future.

After a call to a crisis hotline, I focused on a book by Baron Baptiste, titled *Journey Into Power*, in which Baptiste outlines his "Eight Universal Principles for Stepping Up to the Edge." A quote stuck with me: "All life happens in the present moment; the psychology of growth is being in the process and taking it one moment at a time."

It would be at least a year later before I truly embraced the necessity of taking life one moment at a time. This strategy not only brought me some semblance of peace and sanity in the mini-crises I would continue to experience along the way, but also enabled me to slow down and appreciate all the gifts that were scattered along my journey.

Life is a series of moments that are "now." When you keep your focus on "now," you are not denying the past that led up to this moment or the plans that have yet to be made in future moments, days, weeks and months. You are simply prioritizing your focus into the most manageable time period that exists: the right now. Be aware of everything in this moment and accept it. If it is good, relish it for that moment. If it is painful, know that you are a few moments away from a new and different "now." Let life unfold one "now" at a time.

Are you making a list, talking things out with a friend, or lying in your bed crying? No matter the situation, stop. Close your eyes and take 10 deep breaths. Isolate any thought, feeling or fear that is not in the "right now," and let it go. Bring yourself back into this one moment.

Journey Step 2: Break life into tiny chunks

In crisis, a person is in disequilibrium. That person loses the ability to focus, be organized and think clearly. The mind screams, "What do I do next?" But there is no logical answer. Be assured that in crisis, even the most intelligent and organized person becomes lost, dumbfounded, and feeling as if he or she is drowning. In short, that person loses touch with all that is life and living.

The best thing to do is let go. Let someone else – a family member, crisis specialist or counselor, clergy member, friend or law enforcement officer – walk you through the plan.

Consider an example from my situation. After the initial shock wore off, my main concern was for my two children. What would I tell them? How would I tell them? Had my ex-husband touched them or hurt them? What had they seen? What would happen to child support and all the financial promises made just a year prior to this crisis in the divorce decree? How would my children survive the questions and teasing of other children?

As these questions made my head spin, my mom brought me back into the moment. We sat down and devised a plan for how and when I would talk to the children. As simple as this plan was, I wrote it down for clarity. The children would come home, and I would tell them their father had been arrested. I would explain the charges in the simplest terms and answer any questions they might have. As fearful as I was of the energy and strength this small plan would require, it was a clear plan nonetheless. And in making this plan for the next few moments, I had created my first success in this healing journey.

As time went on, I had to start planning my life again. Yet there were days that someone could ask me to lunch, and it would throw me into a crying frenzy. I couldn't even think a few hours in advance.

How can a victim of betrayal overcome the feeling of being frozen in time? Simple. Break down each day into an hour-by-hour to-do list. By dividing the day into manageable chunks, a person in crisis can deal with everyday challenges while working toward equilibrium.

For so long, I could not make simple decisions. I could not answer, "What would you like for lunch?" without tremendous stress. I could not think about who would take my son to baseball practice the next day. Decisions like these felt equivalent to the decision as to whether I could be a heart donor. As a Type-A personality, I have traditionally been very organized. I'm the crazy woman who writes her grocery list in the order of the grocery store so the shopping experience is handy, clean, quick, neat and convenient. To lose that security blanket in the wake of this crisis, moment by moment, became overwhelming.

Now, several years after the initial crisis, I can finally look at my calendar and plan where I need to be next Monday. My children are thankful for this. It had to be scary for a while when they would need to be places, and I couldn't tell you which end was up. I have very patient children. My son always says, "Go with the flow, Mom." I'm going with God's plan. While I keep a calendar for appointments, I don't plan as far ahead as I used to. I accept that "best-laid plans" generally aren't. I've often been told that if you want to make God laugh, tell Him your plan. For every planned event or activity I have, I now appreciate that something will probably prevent me from carrying it through exactly the way I thought. Go with the flow.

Going with the flow leads me toward my peaceful place. Going with the flow reduces worry. Release the control. Having a plan is fine, as long as you realize it might not happen the way you thought it would. That's real life. Putting together a plan and then grabbing onto it in a chokehold – controlling every moment to the extent you take it as a personal defeat if something in the plan doesn't work – is ridiculous. We don't see it, though, until we step outside of the situation.

I wasn't given a choice. I had to live one moment at a time because, in my crisis, there were so many unknowns. There was nothing neat and clean about this situation. Todd's eventual sentencing, family court and estate issues, the emotional well-being of my children and my emotional healing were all unknowns and works in progress. Only after all of those issues were settled could we begin to live the rest of our lives.

After betrayal, you spend so much time beating yourself up and wondering how you could have missed this. Give yourself permission to plan only one hour at a time. You will set yourself up for victory. Mini-accomplishments, even one hour at a time, help build your inner strength and enable you to work toward equilibrium on this journey home.

Journey Step 3: Talk yourself through the pain

Most people who have experienced deep betrayal are familiar with the cocooning mentioned above. It's much easier to withdraw than to face the world and the problems it presents. During these times, there are powerful strategies that can be used to stay centered in the moment.

First, simply pick up a pen and a journal, and write what you are feeling right now. Oftentimes, after seeing a meaningful quote on a card or email, I would write it at the top of a page in my journal and then note the feelings it stirred in me. Some days, I would start off with a statement like, "I want to curl up and cry in bed today because… " On other days, I would identify a feeling (e.g., betrayed) at the top of the page and just write. How had he betrayed me? How did I feel? The beauty of these journal thoughts is that days, weeks or months later, I could go back and read each one. This would enable me to both identify the feelings I was having at that time and see how far I had come in my healing journey. I dated every entry.

In my journey of healing, I also have kept plenty of inspirational and self-help books on hand. On days when I really needed to step back and take life one moment at a time, I would remove all distractions, curl up in my favorite comfy chair, and read a chapter from one of these books. I limited myself to this "one-chapter-at-a-time" approach to keep the information in manageable chunks. The book subjects included inspirational quotes, spirituality, self-help on grieving or betrayal, and beyond.

One day, I picked up *The Mastery of Love* by Don Miguel Ruiz and turned to the chapter on fear. I immediately grasped a wise thought: "Love has no expectations; fear is filled with expectations." Ruiz's statement on love and fear summarized so clearly what I was feeling at every milestone along my journey. I was filled with expectations about how I *should* be feeling, how I *should* leave my house and rejoin society as I had once known it, and how I *should* be able to forgive Todd for what he had done to me and my children.

I took my journal out and made a list of all the things I feared as they related to this crisis. It was a very long list. I then tore the list out, crumpled it, burned it and prayed to God for help in letting go of my fears. I promised to put my fear into God's hands. I promised that every moment I felt fear, I would remind myself that fear was a lack of faith in God and represented only a set of expectations I held in an effort to control the situation.

I have performed this "burning-away-my-fears" ritual a few times now, and I never fail to feel a complete sense of relief and peace in that moment.

Journey Step 4: Embrace your healing body

My situation often created a sick feeling in the pit of my stomach, made worse by lethargy and absolutely no appetite. The remedy for those nagging symptoms was a combination of meditation and yoga, which also has provided an excellent way to merge my mind, body and spirit in the present moment.

After my divorce, active participation in yoga classes became a significant part of my life. After the day of Todd's arrest, yoga saved my life. Yoga strives to unite the body and the mind, shifting both to a state of equilibrium. This unity, which works to strengthen the body while tapping into your innermost strength, is a tremendously empowering healing tool.

When I first discovered yoga, it was merely an alternative workout option to help me stay fit while recovering from a knee injury. After a couple of months of regular yoga practice, however, I found so much more than just a fit body.

I was practicing "power yoga," a unique combination of different types of yoga. My instructors consistently focused their guiding words on the interaction and flow of every breath with every movement. They also incorporated the gaze and focus in every posture, always urging students to stay in the present moment, be aware of physical and emotional feelings, and then let go to move to the next moment. By combining deep and rhythmic breathing with the slow flow of the body from posture to posture, staying keenly aware of every movement and every point of tension, I was able to free myself during the meditation and yoga practice of all thoughts past and future.

I encourage anyone going through crisis or in the midst of a healing journey to incorporate yoga into their life. In larger cities, it is not difficult to find a multitude of private yoga studios, as well as larger fitness centers that offer yoga classes as a part of their regular schedule. If you live in a smaller town or cannot find a class that suits you, there are a multitude of wonderful videos and DVDs to guide you through home practice. Some of my favorite yoga practitioners include Baron Baptiste, Rodney Yee and Seane Corn.

One of the simplest relaxation techniques is also one of the most amazing and underutilized tools we have: the breath. For years, psychologists have used the breath as a therapeutic tool to reduce stress, diminish anger and increase relaxation.

When I found myself on the verge of a panic attack from fears of the future or an anger attack from the betrayal of the past, I oftentimes put on my headphones. I played my favorite soft music and just breathed. The key to focusing on the "now" is to make yourself perfectly still and breathe.

To gain access to your innermost stillness or peaceful place, find a comfortable spot and lie flat on your back. You might use a yoga mat or towel under you for comfort. With legs fully extended and hip-width distance apart, scan your body from toes to head and relax every muscle. Extend your arms just outside of your hips, palms up. Close your eyes and take deep breaths. Each breath is in through your nose, lips closed and throat soft, and travels to the belly. The exhale takes the breath, slowly and deliberately, back out through the nose. With every inhale, the belly rises; with every exhale, the belly softens and relaxes. Silently and slowly count to four on every inhale, and another four for every exhale.

To get the most out of this deep-breathing exercise, set aside 15 minutes for your "breathing time." Once the four-count breath is established and your body comfortably melts into every inhale and exhale, alert the ears and the mind to the sounds around you. Empty the mind of thoughts of what you ate for breakfast or the afternoon's to-do list. Pay attention only to the sound of your breath and any other subtle sounds in that very moment.

Once you have a good grasp of this exercise, it can become a wonderful part of your healing – a tool you can take wherever you go. When I began to feel panic or fear, particularly surrounding the issues of financial responsibility for the children and the potential for Todd to get out of jail and attempt to see the children against their wishes, I would stop and begin a breathing exercise. With a deeply relaxed body and a peaceful mind, I would use self-affirmations focused only on my *right now*. Todd is in jail *right now*. *Right now*, this month's mortgage is paid. The kids and I are healthy *right now*. After 15 minutes or so, I could emerge with a clear and rational frame of mind, and a relaxed body.

Journey Step 5: Prepare for dark days

As someone who has stood alone and faced the pain of betrayal, I am here to tell you that dark days will happen. Dark days occur when you suddenly feel overwhelmed, panicked and filled with fear, sadness or bewilderment. Don't fight it. Accept it, and allow yourself to live in this moment. Create your Dark-Day Plan and stick with it. Here are some of my personal strategies to help you cope with the darkness:

- Acknowledge that today is a Dark Day and allow yourself to accept it.

- Pull out your journal and read your thoughts, noting progress you have made.

- Take a hot bath, lighting candles and listening to a CD of your favorite songs.

- Cry and be okay with it. Crawl into bed with a big box of tissues and cry loudly. The act of crying or sobbing can be quite cathartic, especially if you are spending so much of your time smiling on the outside with the darkness screaming on the inside.

- Take a walk or attend an exercise class. The adrenaline rush has a positive effect on your mood and improves your feelings about your body.

- Read! After my crisis occurred, I created my own library of inspirational and self-help books. During a dark day, I would grab one of these books off the shelf and read just one chapter for inspiration. Especially useful were books that share stories of victory after crisis or give strategies on how to move toward victory in life.

- Set an ending time for your dark-day rituals. If you need to pick up your kids from school at 3 p.m., allow yourself until then to be with the darkness.

- Take a shower, put on some makeup and get out of the house. Even if I just needed to go to the post office or bank, I made myself walk inside, rather than driving through in my pajamas with my box of tissues.

- Stop all activity immediately upon the initial feelings of panic and go to a quiet place. Situate the kids, pull over to the side of the road, or gracefully get out of a social situation – whatever it takes. Breathe. Just breathe.

Journey Step Summary

1. **Take one moment at a time**

- Focus on now.

- Be aware of what is happening in this moment – and accept it.

- Feeling overwhelmed? Stop, close your eyes, and take 10 deep breaths. Isolate feelings or fears that are not in the "right now," and let them go.

2. **Break life into tiny chunks**

- When in crisis, don't be afraid to let go. Let someone else help you create a plan to address the immediate issues that need attention.

- Write down your plan in simple, manageable steps. Complete these steps to experience an empowering victory.

- Break each day into an hour-by-hour to-do list. This will keep you moving forward with small successes.

- Go with the flow. By releasing worry and control, you will dramatically decrease your stress level.

- Give yourself permission to plan only one hour at a time.

3.   Talk yourself through the pain

- In a journal, write what you are feeling right now.

- Continue using your journal to explore thoughts and feelings each day.

- Assemble a collection of inspirational and self-help books. When you need comfort or assistance, read just one chapter.

- Complete a "burning-away-my-fears" ritual.

4.   Embrace your healing body

- Incorporate yoga into your life.

- Set aside 15 minutes a day for deep-breathing exercises.

5.   Prepare for Dark Days

- Create a Dark-Day Plan and stick with it.

CHAPTER | 9

UNDERSTANDING COLLATERAL DAMAGE

In March 2005, Todd wrote me a letter from his jail cell. His words remain etched into my brain. "I assure you, this is no country club," he said of the federal prison. "I have lost everything – my practice, my airplane, my boat, my kids. I might only serve some time in prison, but in reality I am serving a life sentence."

In his self-pitying diatribe, Todd never once alluded to the damage he had done to so many people in his life – particularly his children. What about the life sentence of his victims and his children, who must live forever with the knowledge of what their father did? For years to come, they must answer questions about their dad to themselves and others. What about the life sentence of his son, who would eventually grapple with the reality that his own father was sexually deviant and abused young boys for his own gratification?

One day, the words just slipped out of my mouth. Collateral damage. This phrase perfectly described the broad community of people harmed by my husband's betrayal. While Austin, Alexa and I were secondary victims of Todd's selfish crimes, so too were a multitude of others who had trusted him. These included our extended family, my children's classmates and their families, our church family, our neighbors, Todd's patients and employees … the list goes on and on.

Betrayal is not about one perpetrator and one victim. Betrayal is a high-intensity hurricane with an overwhelming aftermath. It affects primary victims, secondary victims, all those who came into contact with the perpetrator and all those who come into contact with the victims. Whether we openly admit to the betrayal, work through it privately or try to ignore it doesn't matter. The aftermath exists.

The collateral damage was all around us, living, breathing and needing to find healing. The actions of this child predator left a huge wave in his wake, and the collateral damage was colossal. Every one of these people knew Todd on some level. They were close to him. They believed in him. His actions shook their trust. None of them had chosen this journey, and all would eventually heal. But the emotional scars will remain forever.

In many ways, I felt personally responsible for the pain so many of my close friends and relatives were experiencing during this tragedy. Yet my feelings of humiliation were tempered by the empathy I felt for Todd's other secondary victims.

"How did this happen? Were there any signs?" Todd's father asked me with pleading eyes. More than anybody outside of my own home, Todd's parents suffered. His father's anger was palpable, and his mother's already declining health grew more fragile. In their unimaginable pain, they needed to find some semblance of peace. They struggled for answers that would allow them to continue loving and supporting their son. To accomplish this, they needed to blame someone else, enabling them to break free of the implied relationship between their son's criminal actions and his upbringing.

About a month after Todd's arrest, his mother called to inquire about the children. Things grew tense as the conversation progressed.

"Maybe if you had been a better wife, or if you had built a better marriage, none of this would have happened," she cried in frustration.

Part of me wanted to bite back, unleashing a torrent of evidence that countered her ridiculous accusations. She didn't know about the hidden boxes full of teen magazines with pictures of young male actors. I had never told her about the pictures of a boy from her hometown that Todd kept for so many years. I had shielded her from the piles and piles of porn that were stacked in his cabinets. And even now, I held my tongue, reminding myself that her words came out of bewilderment and pain, not reality. Piling on with more of the sordid details would not heal this woman – or me.

Then there was the staff at Todd's dental office. After his arrest, they remained in the office, answering phones and trying to keep up some semblance of normal behavior. Their kind and courageous actions would make it easier to sell the practice without creating any more damage than had already occurred. One day, I asked them to stop by my home after work. Each greeted me with a warm hug and concerned inquiries about the children.

As I returned their embraces, I realized how clearly I felt their pain as well. Why did so many people have to hurt so badly at the hands of one selfish man? I remember so vividly Todd's most trusted staff member who had served him for so many years as his manager, friend and sounding board. She had allowed her young son to be around Todd on so many occasions. I could see the void in her eyes now and recognized it all too easily. Still drowning in shock and confusion, this wonderful woman had not even hit the point of pain yet. As the years progressed, we occasionally spoke and she revealed to me that she had sought out counseling for her pain. She echoed many of the sentiments I had felt as she questioned her own judgment and ability to trust.

In conversations with both Todd's old acquaintances and my friends, the collateral damage became clear. These caring people were sad and concerned for me and my children. At the same time, they felt angry and betrayed by someone who pretended to be kind and respectful. In many cases, I could hear the unspoken questions that screamed under the surface of our subdued conversations. "Darlene, did you know? How could you have missed this? What if he had molested my son while he was in your care?" All I could do was hug these friends with a heavy heart, apologies repeating over and over in my mind.

My dear father, on the other hand, actually apologized to me. He felt an irrational, but very real, responsibility for introducing me to Todd all those years ago. I assured him that he was not at fault. We all missed seeing Todd's dysfunction. What's more, I reminded Dad, Austin and Alexa would not exist if I had not known Todd.

These children are a privilege and blessing that are worth any cost. My parents so badly wanted to fix the situation and protect their precious grandchildren. Yet they felt helpless, even as their anger burned bright. More difficult than bearing even my own pain was seeing the collateral damage done to Austin and Alexa. At ages 10 and 8, they were overcome by shock and humiliation. They witnessed their mother and their home falling down around them. Suddenly, this man they relied on as their father was in jail for committing horrible crimes. All they had left was trust in their mother, who was struggling to keep herself together.

How could I fix this and make it okay for all those who were in pain? This seemingly impossible challenge was made even more difficult by the silence. As hurt as they were, Todd's secondary victims were reluctant to publicly admit their feelings of betrayal. After all, they thought, this would be akin to conceding they had been fooled.

I had discovered the elephant in the room. The elephant represented pain and betrayal that remained unspoken. Yet those who were hurting and uncomfortable pretended not to see this obvious and gigantic pachyderm, largely because these secondary victims did not want to acknowledge that they had been fooled.

Wherever my children and I went, the elephant blundered through the door. It was our constant visitor at home, school and church. It even squeezed into cars and napped on baseball diamonds. When I had enough of the elephant's intrusions, I was ready to eliminate his presence immediately. I decided to swallow him whole, as opposed to disposing of the elephant bite-by-bite, slowly and meaningfully. Unfortunately, my strategy did not work.

A childhood friend, John, had been through a series of betrayals. He sent an e-mail that put the entire mess into perspective.

"Darlene, the elephant is there, and it is really, really big," John wrote. "Yes, it is bigger than you are. Stop trying to ignore the elephant, and don't even attempt to swallow him whole. Take small bites, one day at a time. Suddenly, one day you will wake up and find that the elephant no longer exists."

Journey Step 6: Eliminate the elephant in the room

The elephant in the room is not the actual betrayal. It is your feelings about the betrayal. In our case, the elephant was humiliation. It took a while for me to slow down and sit in the same room with that elephant, so I could determine how to remove him and my humiliation. To combat these feelings, I emerged from my home and my silence. I chose to speak out about our situation, not with anger, but with grace, peace and a positive message.

My family's story had made national headlines due to the nature of the crime and the FBI sting operation. Just about everyone in the community knew what had happened.

So what if I brought up the topic first, I wondered. This would give others permission to relax and stop walking on eggshells. They would feel free to ask questions, express their thoughts and move on. Immediately, this strategy made me more comfortable in social situations.

Then I received a phone call from a well-known local freelance writer. After initially throwing up barriers, I agreed to an off-the-record conversation with Trey Garrison. Our talk grew personal and emotional, yet it allowed me to find my voice. Suddenly, I felt confident in my message and knew I could communicate with authenticity and integrity.

I agreed to speak with Trey on the record for a story in *D Magazine.* After our interview, I left Trey with a request.

"After you have written the article, please re-read it one last time from the perspective of my young son," I asked. "Make sure that, after he reads it, he will smile and be proud of his mom."

Trey did not disappoint. Published in January 2006, his article was honest, heartfelt and peaceful. This was not the story of a child predator. It was the story of the predator's collateral damage and how all of us would not just survive, but thrive in its wake.

This article was my first little bite out of the elephant in the room. And boy, it felt good. The light at the end of the tunnel was becoming brighter. For all of us.

Journey Step Summary

6.   **Eliminate the elephant in the room**

- Recognize that the elephant is not the actual betrayal.

- Sit quietly with the elephant and uncover what he represents for you.

- Devise a plan to drive the elephant from your life.

Chapter | 10

Relying on Your Own
Firm Foundation

They can be illuminating, painful, even terrifying. Yet along our individual journeys, nobody can escape powerful life lessons. Each time we are asked to choose between two options, a potential life lesson looms. And when overwhelmed by a crisis situation such as betrayal, each person has a particularly critical choice to make. Should you learn from the lessons presented, no matter how difficult the process? Or should you ignore those lessons, running the risks they may be repeated again and again?

Each individual makes a choice based on personal life philosophies or belief systems. By choosing to learn from the crisis, despite the pain, you can create defining moments. In turn, these moments can become stepping stones that lead closer to the very essence of you. You can "come home," becoming and understanding who you are in your truest, purest and most authentic form. Home is the beginning and end of the journey, resulting in self-knowledge, love and acceptance.

But where exactly do personal life philosophies come from? You could ask this question of 10 different people and receive 10 unique responses.

We are not born with life philosophies. Our views of life are influenced by our parents, our siblings, our friends, our spiritual beliefs, our personal experiences and the books we read.

As a part of my therapeutic healing, I took an emotional and mental journey back to my childhood. This enabled me to examine the influences of both nature and nurture on how I approach life's lessons. Why had I developed my personal life philosophies, and how was this affecting my ability to heal? In one case, reading a book dramatically changed the way I viewed myself and my life.

In May 2006, I was struggling to find my way spiritually, emotionally, and as the sole financial and emotional provider for my two children. I ran across an excerpt from T.D. Jakes' beautiful book, *Mama Made the Difference*. In an instant, I was empowered to believe in myself, to pray and to endure. Jakes writes, "If there is one thing a mother is not, it's a quitter. No, a mother will persevere for the sake of those she loves. She will scale the most rugged of mountains, leap the highest of obstacles and keep walking through the darkest of nights because of her love for her children."

Wow, Pastor Jakes knew me better than I knew myself.

His book made me examine my own parents and their influence on me, not just as a child but as the woman I was trying to understand today. For example, my dad taught me a simple yet powerful lesson: be yourself. This was exemplified in his own life, thanks to his honesty, sincerity and down-to-earth nature. When my father retired from his long career as a bank executive, his co-workers did not praise his excellent loan decisions or savvy business acumen, no matter how deserving he may have been of such accolades. Rather, they complimented my father for his kind, caring, fun and concerned personality. No matter the adversity, Dad was always consistent in these qualities. To this day, when my mom becomes frustrated with me, she declares, "You're just like your father!" I consider it the highest compliment. While I wish I had automatically inherited my dad's expressive brand of honesty and sincerity, these ideas had to be observed, pondered and appreciated before I could incorporate them into my personal value system to their fullest extent.

My mom taught me perseverance under any and all circumstances – even when those close to you question your actions. Raised in a traditional Lebanese household, my mother was raised to believe that a woman's first priority was caring for her husband and children. She was a schoolteacher when she met and married my dad. When I was born, my mom retired to raise her family, which ultimately included three children.

For years, Mom dreamed of earning a counseling degree and opening a private practice. My very traditional grandfather chided her for wanting to return to school while raising three young children. But with support from my grandmother, father and many friends, my mother pursued and accomplished her dream. I watched my mother break free from her identification solely as a wife and mother, expanding into a college post-graduate, business owner and advocate for children. Despite cultural stigmas and the sheer exhaustion of filling so many roles as wife, mother and student, Mom never gave up. In the end, my grandfather even became one of her greatest fans and supporters. Her determination, coupled with my Dad's undying support for her, are precious gifts to me. They have served as role models as I have carried my children through tremendous difficulty.

My parents also taught me the importance of family, and that we stick together through tough times. Needless to say, when Todd was arrested, my first phone call was to my dad. From the time I arrived home that day, I was surrounded by my parents, siblings and other family members who helped with the children – and helped me pick up the pieces.

Friends have helped shape my life philosophies as well. The mother of five children, including a set of twins, my friend Michelle taught me the healing power of laughter, and how to laugh through tears. Michelle showed me how to trust a friend, as well as how to be trusted. She exemplifies grace and Christian love.

Journey Step 7: Identify your personal life philosophies

There I sat in my therapist's office, mulling over the strong, positive influences of my family and friends. Yet what did I discover? Despite this positive background, I was never comfortable in my own skin.

I spent much of my childhood and early life trying to re-define myself. Being overweight during childhood led me to be insecure and defensive in relationships. What's more, I had developed a skewed view of success. Success, I had decided, was being thin. It also came to those who were thin. Failure, on the other hand, directly resulted from being overweight.

I had allowed this twisted thinking to completely obscure my true life philosophies. So I set about uncovering what I truly believed. Try taking this journey with me.

Get seven pieces of paper, or set aside seven pages in your journal. At the top of each page, write one of the following words: faith, parents, success, failure, love, trust and courage. On each page, simply write your thoughts about each word. Give your opinions. Name a person who exemplifies each word.

The next day, go back and read each entry. Identify which parts of your writing truly resonate with your soul. Ferret out ideas that are misguided or not representative of your spirit.

For example, when I completed this exercise, I was amazed by how easily I could suddenly identify the wrong-headed ideas that were not part of my true self. Rather, they were part of the public façade I had built over the years. Once I understood these ideas – and how wrong they were for me – I simply threw them away.

The thoughts and ideas that came from the deepest part of my soul are carefully recorded, stapled and tucked into one of my journals. Occasionally, I pull these out and review them to ensure I am continuing to be truly authentic with myself and others.

Journey Step 8: Express gratitude for the gifts God has given that make you happy

On a day that I felt particularly overwhelmed, I sat in the bathtub crying as though my heart would never heal. Tired of wallowing in self-pity, I decided to focus on gratitude by enumerating everything that made me happy. I began writing down only those gifts that God had a hand in bestowing. That way, the gifts would be pure, true, lasting and real. As I made my list, the money, big house, airplane and boat meant nothing to me. I focused on those things that really mattered:

- Austin

- Alexa

- a loving extended family

- true friends

- cool green grass beneath my bare feet on a warm summer day

- the smell of rain before it arrives

- the sound of ocean waves crashing on the shore

- laughter

The purpose of the list? It was the first year after our tragedy. Each day, I felt as if I were simply going through the motions. It was easy to fall into a negative rut. This list inspired me. I read it every day to find joy in my life. As time passed, I needed the list as a crutch less and less. Yet I still added to it when I felt profound gratitude for one of God's creations.

Today, my list has grown long. It increases monthly, and nothing has ever been crossed off.

Begin your own gratitude list. Use it to focus on the positive, profound gifts in your life. By dwelling on these wonderful things, you can more easily let go of the circumstances that have caused you pain. What's more, your list can put smile on your face and create a grateful heart prepared to move into the future.

Journey Step 9: Make faith a daily part of your journey

Through this process, my greatest lessons have come from God.

It took a series of life lessons during my 20s and 30s before I realized that I was ignoring the bigger picture. I struggled with an eating disorder in college. I lost a dear friend to suicide just before I embarked on a new career. Most difficult of all, I almost lost my son at age 7 to a rare side-effect of staph pneumonia.

As my marriage continued to deteriorate after Austin's illness, I realized there were two completely different people living as Darlene. One was my true self. The other was the Darlene I

Journey Step Summary

7. **Identify your personal life philosophies**

    - Get seven pieces of paper, or set aside seven pages in your journal.

    - At the top of each page, write one of the following words: faith, parents, success, failure, love, trust and courage.

    - On each page, write your thoughts about the word. Give your opinions. Name a person who exemplifies the word.

    - The next day, go back and read each entry.

    - Identify which ideas resonate with your soul. Remove ideas that are misguided or not representative of your spirit.

    - When working through challenges, return to these pages. Embrace your spirit, and avoid those actions and behaviors not consistent with your personal life philosophies.

8. **Express gratitude for the gifts God has given that make you happy**

    - Begin a list of things that make you happy. Only include those items that are gifts from God.

    - As time passes, add to the list.

    - When you feel challenged, review the list and embrace the gifts in your life.

9.   Make faith a daily part of your journey

- Create a virtual shoebox. When you are hurting, pray. Take the one item that is causing the most pain and give it up to God. Put it in the shoebox, and place the box on a high closet shelf. Only touch the shoebox to put another pain or worry inside. Never, under any circumstance, take something back out of the box.

- Find meaningful ways to connect with your faith, such as daily prayers, personal Bible lessons and group Bible studies.

- Go on walks with God for quiet time, prayer and meditation.

CHAPTER | 11

TRUE HEALING AFTER BETRAYAL

There I stood, at the door to my new life, trying to establish my new normal. God had set the path, but it was still fuzzy to me. The way was most certainly not straight or simple.

I was terrified, and my fears kept taking hold. What if I could not provide financially for my children? What if I was not strong enough to help them emotionally heal? Yet I was fortunate that Austin and Alexa took hold of my hands. With courage and trust, they prodded me forward on our path. Ready or not.

The first thing I noticed was my incredible lack of balance. Body, mind and spirit were in disequilibrium. Ironically, even though I was a yoga instructor who preached balance in all things, I had been thrown totally out of whack. It was time to find my personal synchronicity.

My faith enveloped me in a shroud of peace, and I resumed yoga practice to keep me there. When not having conversations with God, I spent a lot of my quiet time meditating and using visualization to "see" myself living and loving with grace and peace.

One of my greatest challenges was patience.

"It is time to be better - right now," I would complain to my therapist, John.

"Be patient with the grief, the pain and the emotional rollercoaster," he would answer.

"I'm so tired of these feelings," I would vent to my mother. "Patience is a virtue," she replied. "Time heals all wounds." Yes, their answers seemed too pat, too hokey, too canned. Yet, in the end, they were too true.

I bought patience by picking up a pen, writing journal entries and answers to specific questions.

Journey Step 10: Define your circle of support and strategic alliances

I spent hours listing all of the people who had been true, genuine and supportive in our recovery process. My immediate circle of support included my family and a few dear friends. Amazingly enough, however, the list did not include several people whom I had considered close companions in the past. I realized early on that this was a very public and messy topic. Some people preferred that I kick it under the carpet and never discuss it again. I understand their discomfort, but that was not how I was choosing to recover.

On the flip side, a few folks I had considered only casual friends were quick to react. They stayed by our sides through the toughest of times. Our friendships grew, as did my circle of support. To this day, I have wonderful people appear in my life at just the right time, with the words or actions I need most at that moment. I am blessed to have had my eyes opened wide, so I can see these amazing angels on Earth.

Once my circle of support list was compiled, I created a strategic alliances list. It included my therapist, Victims Outreach, Dallas Children's Advocacy Center, my friend Paige Flink at The Family Place (one of many amazing Dallas organizations that serve victims of domestic violence), and a host of Internet resources. I created a master list of these alliances customized for my crisis and recovery. I still keep that list in my home office for easy reference whenever I need it.

My strategic alliance list gives me tremendous confidence and peace during times of disequilibrium. At times, I become overly anxious or feel overwhelmed. I pull out the list and read the names of the wonderfully supportive people and organizations that are part of my team. That alone can bring me back into equilibrium. What's more, I have used this list to make referrals for other women in crisis, giving my strategic alliances the ability to help even more people in need.

Journey Step 11: Face the details with eyes wide open

Up to this point, I had dealt with my emotions without confronting the details of my ex-husband's crimes. I was in a kind of continuous denial. Once I realized the extent of my willful blindness, I decided to face the grim details. I would learn the whos, hows and whys of pedophiles and child predators. In addition, I was ready to know all the facts of Todd's particular case.

A year, several motions and many court dates later, I sat down in front of my computer one evening and read.

I scoured the blogs. I researched NAMBLA in horror. I read all of the national articles from the date of Todd's arrest. I read transcripts from news programs that had covered the case, such as the *The O'Reilly Factor.* I scanned transcripts and motions from Todd's court appearances. I reviewed Todd's credit card statement listing the fees and meals at the NAMBLA convention where he planned the trip to Mexico for sex with minor boys.

Hours later, I emerged from my study ready to speak out to anyone who would listen.

God's path for me was clearer. I just needed to find the means to taking that path. I would be patient and stay the course fearlessly. I could not wait to talk to the children about this—not the details of this mortifying case, but about my desire to speak out and protect other children. I would not speak out to the public without their clear understanding and blessing. This was their story, their lives, too.

Of course, every betrayal is unique. Many victims of betrayal feel pain and humiliation, leading them to second-guess their own actions and harshly judge themselves. Ultimately, a large number of these victims suffer in silence, choosing to kick the issue under the carpet and ignore it.

While initially attractive, this strategy simply does not work. When not exposed to the light of day, betrayals continue to haunt their victims like a monster under the bed. I cannot encourage you enough to speak out about your experiences.

Consider the mother who loses a child to suicide. Somehow, amid her profound grief, she starts an organization to help the secondary victims of suicide. While her message and strength are empowering to her audiences, they also serve to:

- take the elephant out of the room

- serve as a therapeutic way for the secondary victim to work through the pain

- help others in need

To whom should you speak? Anyone who will listen. This might include:

- community organizations that would benefit from your story and message

- other victims who have gone through a similar betrayal and feel alone

- blogs or web sites that might reach people facing similar issues

As you face the details, keep something in mind. You may come to understand what happened to you, and even why it happened. Or, you may never truly understand the causes of your betrayal. Even if you do understand, that fact alone will not eliminate the pain. At some point, acceptance becomes more important than understanding.

Journey Step 12: Lists and letters

Facing the situation gave me power. Yet at the same time, the pain was intense.

My friends kept labeling me as "courageous" and "strong." I came to realize, however, that my courage and strength lay in an ability to face the pain without fear. I had to shore up this ability, so I would not buckle in harder circumstances.

I began this fortification by creating a list of unknowns. My list had four columns: a check box, the unknown item, a space for "control" and a space for "no control." First, I listed everything I considered an unknown, such as:

- a job that would financially secure my children's future

- Todd's sentencing hearing

- Todd's status in the kids' lives after his release

- forgiving Todd for what he had done to our family

I went back through the list, choosing between "control" and "no control" for each item. This exercise was huge for me. It gave me direction, just by virtue of making the list. When I saw that I had control over a particular item on the list, I took steps to positively affect the outcome. When I designated an item as something over which I had no control, I filed it away mentally. This alone reduced my daily stress level, as I chose to stop fretting about the unknowns I could not control. As time passed, each item would be checked off once it was no longer "unknown" status. By managing this list, I could manage my outlook and understanding of my situation.

Next, I reverted back to a wonderful exercise I used in my professional career to help abused children. With my gentle assistance, the child would write a letter to the person who hurt him or her. I assured the child that the letter would never be sent. They were simply using words and pictures for cathartic release. At the end of the exercise, we would discuss the letter before tearing it into many tiny pieces.

It was time for the therapist to take her own advice. I wrote Todd the letter I would never send. I covered three pages with my frustrations, anger and betrayal. I re-read it. There it was, my heart and soul, in black and white: "I hate you for this. I hate what you have done to our children and their future. I couldn't spot your sick ways or the betrayal from a mile away, much less lying next to you in bed for 10 years. How could I have missed this? How will I ever trust my heart again?"

I tore the papers up into many tiny pieces and burned them to ashes. No more being a victim. It was time to be a victor. I had handled the crisis. I had stared down the unknown. Now, it was time to look forward. I longed to speak publicly. I sat the children down and explained what I wanted to speak out about, who I might be speaking to, and what difference it might make in helping others.

"Will you be famous?" my daughter, then age nine, wanted to know.

I laughed and told her this was not how I imagined being famous. "When I was a little girl," I said, "I dreamed of being a rock star like Joan Jett or Pat Benatar."

"Why do you need to help other people fight predators? Where were all those people when we needed help?" interjected my son Austin. He was a little man of few words. When he spoke, it commanded my attention. I explained that his concerns were the very reason I needed to speak out.

"This type of thing is happening all over the country, but people don't like to talk about it," I said. "They feel humiliated, or think it's just too hard to talk about in public. But if I speak out, we could offer comfort and courage to other families that have been hurt. More people will start talking about it and taking action, and we can save children's lives. We can also help people who go through this type of crisis to heal and get better, like your Mom did, so that I could take care of you."

"Do you really think you can make a difference, Mom? How can just one person make a difference?" Austin prodded.

"I have some opportunities to speak on television to very large audiences," I said. "Yes, I think we can make a difference." I also told him about the talks I would be giving with Dallas Children's Advocacy Center to help parents, grandparents and others who are in contact with children to better know how to protect kids from this kind of crime. My intellectually driven son understood and was on board.

Several of my appearances were quite memorable. I wasn't just making a difference in the lives of other children, I was empowering myself as part of my own betrayal recovery.

When Deborah Roberts came into my home to interview me for a *20/20* segment, we had to stop mid-way through the interview to change tapes.

"Wow. I'm a Mom, too, and this is pretty powerful stuff," she said with tears in her eyes. "It really makes you take a hard look at protecting your kids." She was a talented professional who, on that day, conducted an interview as a mom first. That made the story even more appealing and powerful to audiences.

When Harpo Productions called my home, I initially declined to make an appearance on *The Oprah Winfrey Show*. While Oprah is a powerful force around the globe, I feared being portrayed as a victim. Then, one of her producers called and asked me to appear on a show exposing NAMBLA to the public. Other guests would include Chris Hansen of Dateline NBC's *To Catch a Predator* series, as well as the FBI agent, Robert Hamer, who had gone undercover in NAMBLA to expose the organization and make arrests of those members who were acting upon their urges with minor boys.

I appeared on the show in September 2006. I still get chills when I watch a tape of Ms. Winfrey's opening segment. The most moving moment for me, however, came when I had a few moments alone with Agent Hamer seeking answers to a few of my unknowns. I wanted to check them off my list. I asked about his memories and interactions with Todd. I asked if Todd ever talked about having a wife and kids. Then I asked how long Todd had been a member of NAMBLA. Despite my gut feeling and Todd's confession about prior incidences of child molestation before our marriage, I was hoping to hear differently. Agent Hamer confirmed that Todd had been in NAMBLA since prior to our wedding date. There it was – no longer an unknown.

I continued speaking out to church and school organizations and by partnering with the Dallas Children's Advocacy's Education Outreach Program. With each presentation, I grew a bit stronger. I wanted to do even more to make a difference. My mind had moved into balance with my faith.

Now it was time to bring a body that had endured physical shock, exhaustion and severe stress into the balance equation.

Journey Step 13: H.E.A.L. to be Real

H.E.A.L. to be Real is my own version of practical therapy.

H: Hug and touch. When it is gentle, the human touch has a calming, soothing element. I wanted to hug and be hugged. I wanted to be held and told everything eventually would be okay. I gave full embrace hugs, holding on to friends and family to thank them for their love and support and, in turn, to physically feel their love and support. I hugged my children a lot more than they were already accustomed to. I wanted them to know touch as a positive, wonderful, healing thing. I wanted them to feel security.

E: Exercise and eat healthy. I didn't need a diet, but I did need to eat. I didn't need a formalized fitness regimen, but I did need to move. At the time of Todd's arrest, I was not out of shape. I was actually at my all-time thinnest. I knew, however, that my body needed nutrients, and moving would trigger endorphins that would aid in reducing stress and keeping my blood pressure and heart healthy.

I had acquired the habit of drinking two glasses of wine almost every evening. This had served as the perfect numbing agent, but wreaked havoc with my sleep patterns. I replaced the wine with lots of water and yoga. I ate fresh fruits and vegetables. I decided that I was permitted to cry any time, as long as I was in motion. Needless to say, my walks with God increased. I became a regular at the YMCA's spin class, huddled in the back of the room and riding with swollen eyes and a runny nose. The instructor, a dear friend of mine, let me cycle the pain and anger away with tears streaming down my cheeks.

A: Ask for – and accept – help. Now was not the time to be Supermom. I spent hours in appointments with attorneys and therapists. As a result, I needed help getting the kids to and from school and their various activities. Some things around the house needed to be done, and I simply had not gotten around to them. I needed to be a high-touch, quality Mom, rather than an "I need to be at everything or I'm horrible" Mom.

L: Laugh and smile a lot. It takes a great deal of courage to cry and be okay with it. It takes even more courage to smile and laugh when you don't want to. I was known for my smile, not to mention that I had always been the funny and warm Darlene to so many people. I had cried so hard for so many months, I was sure my face was frozen in cry-formation. Then, one day, my dear friend Michelle made a light joke about Todd. I laughed so hard that I cried. Those were good tears. After that, I found myself able to approach this heavy, dark topic with a bit of light humor. Usually, this caught the person with whom I was talking off guard. Yet it almost immediately removed the elephant in the room and opened the door to a more lighthearted conversation. It wasn't long before I was laughing often and meaning it. The greatest gift I could give to Austin and Alexa was their smiling, laughing Mom back. That was their sign that everything was going to be okay.

On my bathroom mirror, I hung a quote by French author and philosopher Albert Camus as a daily reminder: "In the depth of winter, I finally learned that within me there lay an invincible summer." Summer, with all its warmth, beauty, fun and freedom, was alive inside of me. I was determined to bring that to my children and anyone with whom I came into contact.

Another author, Glenda Cloud, wrote, "Change is inevitable, growth is intentional." I was close to achieving balance in my mind, body and spirit, and I wanted to be intentional. Change is uncomfortable. It can include doubt, fear and pain, but growth is a choice. I was shouting that choice from the mountaintops!

Anyone who recovers from a betrayal crisis is like a diamond. It begins as a plain piece of coal, emerging as a diamond only after the long journey of heat, pressure and stress. We are all diamonds in the rough. Betrayal and its journey of recovery provide the heat, pressure and stress necessary for our emergence as precious gems.

The irony of this metaphor? The most precious and expensive gem I had owned was the diamond in my engagement ring. This beautiful jewel also represented the darkest time in my life. I struggled with what to do with the diamond. Then, I decided to polish it and change its setting. I couldn't eliminate that dark part of my life, as it resulted in the two most precious gifts God has ever given me: my children. But I could change the setting and its appearance. I made it a solitaire to represent me on my own, in a new setting, still a jewel ... just different. In essence, it represents for me my wealthiest, most precious gem. It stands for my soul. My "home."

Journey Step Summary

10.   **Define your circle of support and strategic alliances**

- List all of the people who have been true, genuine and supportive as you have dealt with betrayal.

- Accept that not everyone you once considered a close friend will be on the list.

- Create a list of strategic alliances, including doctors, therapists, organizations and Internet resources.

- Keep these lists handy for reference.

11.   **Face the details with eyes wide open**

- Learn as much as you can about your specific betrayal.

- Find out more about that type of crime or betrayal in general, so you can find resources to help you and avoid similar circumstances in the future.

- Reach out to others in your same situation.

- Speak out.

12.   **Lists and letters**

- Create a list of unknowns.

- Categorize each unknown as something you can or cannot control.

- Check off each item as it reaches "known" status.

- Write a letter to your betrayer, detailing your frustrations, anger, thoughts and hurts.

- Destroy the letter.

- Again, find ways to speak out.

13.   H.E.A.L to be Real

- Hug and touch.

- Exercise and eat healthy.

- Ask for – and accept – help.

- Laugh and smile a lot.

CHAPTER | 12

FINDING THE SILVER LINING – INSIDE AND OUT

It had been about a year since Todd's arrest. At last, I began to experience some emotional stability. As his sentencing quickly approached, I had to face two high hurdles: forgiveness and trust.

Forgiveness was not just about Todd. Even harder, could I forgive myself? How could I not have seen *something*, sensed *something*? There was so much collateral damage in this mess. Could I have prevented all this pain that so many, especially my own two children, were experiencing? I asked myself those questions on a daily basis. But it was time to stop apologizing. Even though none of this was my fault, I felt an allegiance to a community of family and friends. I was the person who could ease the healing and, hopefully, help others by speaking out. I could educate and empower them and, just maybe, we could protect children and communities with the lessons I had learned.

Could I forgive Todd? Even if I made the decision to forgive from my intellectual self, how could I emotionally forgive him? And what exactly did I need to forgive?

I came to understand a new meaning of forgiveness. It did not mean that I was not angry about how he damaged our children emotionally. It did not mean that I excused him or condoned his behavior. It merely meant I could let go of the situation, so that I could let go of my suffering.

Now that I had completely over-thought the forgiveness of Todd, I decided to take some tangible actions for the ultimate "letting go." After sitting in jail since his initial arrest, Todd finally would be sentenced in May 2006 in San Diego. I would be there. I needed to look him in the eyes one last time before letting the pain go. With my counselor's encouragement, I wrote a victim statement for his sentencing. Because I was a secondary victim, I knew that my statement likely would not be allowed. Nevertheless, I wrote it for therapeutic reasons.

I tearfully penned my statement and then read it aloud in a quiet room. I imagined that Todd was sitting across from me, listening to my passionate address. At the end of the statement, I read, "Todd, I cannot forgive you for Austin and Alexa. They will have to do this in their own time and in their own way. I can, however, forgive you for me. Not because I want to, but because I must in order to heal and be the best mom that I can be."

I imagined him staring blankly at me, then looking at his feet. No words, no tearful goodbyes. I then turned around and walked out of that quiet room. I left my images of Todd and all the pain of forgiveness in there, never to be revisited.

Just a week later, I sat in the front row of a San Diego courtroom, directly behind the U.S. attorney who was trying the case. Todd's family sat a few rows back, behind the defense attorney. They were not expecting me to attend, nor was Todd. There was so much I wanted to say to him. I wanted him to know and understand the pain he had caused to countless people. He was pale, thin and void of any emotion. I listened to his much-rehearsed and scripted appeal to the judge, whining that he had "lost everything" and "paid a dear price." Despite my disgust, I forgave him.

This was the end of the road for Todd. But it was the beginning of a new life for me and my kids. The judge sentenced Todd to 24 months in federal prison, followed by the maximum 12 years of supervised release. Todd already had served some of this time, so he was scheduled to walk out of prison in November 2007. The judge also ruled that Todd could have no access to Austin and Alexa until after the 12 years elapsed, and only then if the kids initiated contact. At last, I found forgiveness and peace.

I could not get to the airport fast enough. I wanted to

go home to the kids and start living. But my definition of living included just one last missing element: trust.

I spent the next few hours pondering trust. I knew, without hesitation, that I trusted God. But how could I ever trust another man? And how could I trust myself and the decisions I made based on my heart? I took a long, hard look inside of myself. I analyzed my previous patterns when it came to trust and relationships. I decided to write it all down and face the music.

I described each and every one of my past romantic relationships. I uncovered ugly trends: insecurities, and a desire to be accepted that led me to respond to any man who showed me attention. I didn't like the patterns I was uncovering, yet I knew these were patterns I could control. I could avoid men forever, continue to make the same bad choices, or break free with a new level of trust in my spirituality and myself.

I would never again launch a new romantic relationship simply to fill a void. Rather, I chose a purpose for my life. I would fearlessly create a world where it was okay to be fragile, to be strong, to be honest and to be real. Anyone who entered this world would be shown no false pretenses. This is me. Take it or leave it. I surrendered and left the rest up to the Man with a plan.

God had given this crisis to me, Austin and Alexa as a gift.

Over the next six months, Todd was thoroughly evaluated by a psychiatrist and given a risk level of four. This is the highest risk level for sexual predators and labels them as sexually violent. These individuals have impaired judgment or control, paired with sexual or violent compulsions. This may be the result of pedophilia, another disorder of sexual attraction, mental illness or a personality disorder that distorts thinking, interferes with behavioral control, and predisposes the person to acts of predatory sexual violence.

Just a year and a half earlier, this predator had created a darkness inside of me that I was sure could never heal. The darkness brought a pain that was mind-boggling. And then, over the course of time, prayer, therapy and forgiveness, the darkness began to shrink. Eventually, I re-shaped the darkness into a little black box, tied it with a bright pink ribbon, and stored it on a high shelf in the depths of my soul. My darkness was now a gift. By embracing it as a gift and blessing, I was empowered to help others, starting with my own kids, and live life to its fullest!

I have often been asked if I regret the day I met Phillip Todd Calvin. Without hesitation, I answer, "Absolutely not." I may have pain and sadness, but I also have Austin and Alexa, the products of that meeting. It is my privilege to guide them from childhood through adolescence and into adulthood, teaching them forgiveness, compassion and grace. In every tragedy, there is a silver lining. This tragedy has two silver linings named Austin and Alexa, and they sit at the top of a long list of blessings. These two precious gifts will not merely survive, but thrive. They will thrive not because of, but in spite of, the choices made by Todd Calvin.

Todd was caught before he could bring any physical harm to my children or their friends. A violent predator was identified and confined. I am more spiritually centered than ever, and I have learned what is truly important:

- how to let things go

- how to speak out

- how to dissolve the elephant in the room

- how to be a true friend

I have been blessed to know others' stories of crisis and betrayal, and forged alliances and friendships with so many people I otherwise might not have been privileged to meet. I have found the true, real and authentic me, and love what I found!

One of my favorite quotes was recently published in a book called *She...* by Kobi Yamada. "She not only saw a light at the end of the tunnel, she became that light for others."

Somewhere inside of this amazing journey through pain and recovery, I moved from total darkness. I saw the light at the end of the tunnel, and allowed my own light to shine for myself, my children and others.

I am a woman with vision and dreams. I am a high-touch woman who handwrites personal thank-you notes, prefers a phone call to a text message, and lives her life focused on people. I live with purpose and love with passion. I have identified my natural highs. I strive to walk through every day of my life seeing and experiencing these highs with eyes wide open. I laugh and cherish the laughter of my children. I love the smell of rain. I relish the feel of cool, green grass beneath my bare feet. I love singing at the top of my lungs in my car, windows down, with my best friend. Curling up with hot chocolate in front of a crackling fireplace is a favorite pastime.

I am a light, one of many lights yet to be ignited on this earth.

You are a light as well. Find it and embrace it. You have a purpose and all the tools and resources you need to fulfill that purpose. But you have to decide what to do with those tools and resources. Just as the light is inside of you, so are the answers. Eyes wide open, listen and trust.

Ready, set, go!

AFTERWORD
THE JOURNEY CONTINUES

It was Labor Day weekend in 2003 when I joined Michelle and her mom, Jane, in New York to attend the U.S. Open. I had played and watched tennis since the tender age of four, but this weekend was really just to get my mind off my troubles. Todd and I had filed for divorce just three weeks before, and he was finally moving out of the house. Austin and Alexa were with my parents, and I was sent off by my loved ones to wind down before things got tough in the throes of divorce.

I was emotional most of the trip, trying to come to grips with a failed marriage, as well as a feeling of personal failure. During one of our lovely New York dinners, the subject of nicknames came up. Jane revealed the nickname she had always called Michelle, and I teased her that I wanted a nickname too. Without skipping a beat, Jane lovingly said her nickname for me would be "butterfly." I was finally emerging out of a cocoon of sadness into the woman I was always meant to be. That woman lived inside of me, but only now was I giving her permission to come out. Jane was an amazingly insightful woman that evening, and I wished that I could see in myself what was so evident to her.

Little did any of us know that, 16 months later, this butterfly would begin a journey high and far.

Make no mistake, the journey of betrayal recovery never

truly ends. It merely takes on new forms, moving from pain through healing into living on purpose, with purpose. I am often asked if the pain is still there. Absolutely, it is. Mostly, the pain is out of love for my children. No mother wants to see her children hurt. But I also celebrate the pain because it was my catalyst to the woman I am today. With change come fear, discomfort and disequilibrium. But with change also comes movement. With movement comes growth. With growth comes truly knowing and loving ourselves for who we are—the good, the bad and the ugly—so that we can love others.

Did I ever learn how to trust again? In October 2007, I married a wonderful man named Scott Ellison. I assure you, my journey of learning to trust again did not come easily to me or to him. But he stuck with it, determined to love me and my kids for a lifetime. Yes, I was skeptical. I spent more time looking for signs from God that Scott was not "the one" than I did seeing that Scott was my sign that it was time to move on.

In Scott, I have found all those things I never had in my first marriage. I feel valued and appreciated as a wife. I have a husband who actually wants to be at my children's activities and has so much to offer to the kids in love and wisdom. I feel secure in my marriage, both good days and bad. With Scott come warmth, comfort and unconditional love to which I am still becoming accustomed.

Austin is now in high school, with Alexa not far behind. While I realize that there might be a few bumps in the road ahead because of their biological father's choices, I am confident that they are taking away some amazing life lessons.

In January 2007, Todd filed a motion to reduce child support and other financial obligations to our children. He took this action even though the judge in his criminal case had chosen not to impose a fine because of his "very substantial financial commitments" to our family. The sale of Todd's home, airplane, sailboat and dental practice had generated significant cash, which I had placed in a brokerage account on his behalf. Yet Todd and his parents claimed he would need all of that money for attorney fees and a "decent" lifestyle.

Todd's actions made a decision even easier for my children. In early 2007, the children chose to terminate Todd's parental rights. While the court documents were more than sufficient to keep

Todd at bay as the children grew up, this step provided closure for the kids. I, as well as their own attorney, carefully explained what termination meant. Amazingly enough, the day I went to court to sign the final documents, I noticed that both children seemed to have lighter hearts and more laughter in their lives. Yes, they had to work through their own trust issues when Scott entered their lives. But I am a proud momma when I report that they truly are thriving.

Where I used to define the kids' happiness by their good grades, the sports they played or the friends they hung out with, now happiness is simply revealed in their smiles and anticipation of their lives ahead.

The greatest sign of their healing came one day when, after completing the proposal for this book, I announced that it was ready to go. I reassured the kids that they need not worry about their identities being broadcast to the world because I had not used their names. My son looked at me quizzically and asked, "Why not?" I explained that at their ages, I totally understood if they wanted to remain unidentified. His mature response amazed me. "But it's our story, too." No angst or darkness, just a matter-of-fact statement about the hand he'd been dealt in this life.

Needless to say, I immediately wrote Austin and Alexa back into the book. I am so very proud of the young man and young woman Scott and I have been given the privilege to raise.

As for me, I have a wonderful job in business development, and I have added the job titles of author and motivator. I raise kids, work hard, speak and write about the things that matter most in my life ... and I love every minute of it. I spend a great deal of time creating and helping others develop high-touch alliances — a way of living, doing business and building relationships that is about people connecting with people, despite adversity and challenges.

Oh, one more thing. I used to think of myself as innovative because I could "look outside the box." It was only after my story unfolded that I made the most dramatic of realizations. There is no box.

APPENDIX – A

THE JOURNEY STEPS

1. **Take one moment at a time**

   - Focus on now.

   - Be aware of what is happening in this moment – and accept it.

   - Feeling overwhelmed? Stop, close your eyes, and take 10 deep breaths. Isolate feelings or fears that are not in the "right now," and let them go.

2. **Break life into tiny chunks**

   - When in crisis, don't be afraid to let go. Let someone else help you create a plan to address the immediate issues that need attention.

   - Write down your plan in simple, manageable steps. Complete these steps to experience an empowering victory.

   - Break each day into an hour-by-hour to-do list. This will keep you moving forward with small successes.

- Go with the flow. By releasing worry and control, you will dramatically decrease your stress level.

- Give yourself permission to plan only five minutes at a time.

3. **Talk yourself through the pain**

- In a journal, write what you are feeling right now.

- Continue using your journal to explore thoughts and feelings each day.

- Assemble a collection of inspirational and self-help books. When you need comfort or assistance, read just one chapter.

- Complete a "burning-away-my-fears" ritual.

4. **Embrace your healing body**

- Incorporate yoga into your life.

- Set aside 15 minutes a day for deep-breathing exercises.

5. **Prepare for dark days**

- Create a Dark-Day Plan and stick with it.

6. **Eliminate the elephant in the room**

- Recognize that the elephant is not the actual betrayal.

- Sit quietly with the elephant and uncover what he represents for you.

- Devise a plan to drive the elephant from your life.

7.   **Identify your personal life philosophies**

- Get seven pieces of paper, or set aside seven pages in your journal.

- At the top of each page, write one of the following words: faith, parents, success, failure, love, trust and courage.

- On each page, write your thoughts about the word. Give your opinions. Name a person who exemplifies the word.

- The next day, go back and read each entry.

- Identify which ideas resonate with your soul. Remove ideas that are misguided or not representative of your spirit.

- When working through challenges, return to these pages. Embrace your spirit, and avoid those actions and behaviors not consistent with your personal life philosophies.

8.   **Express gratitude for the gifts God has given that make you happy**

- Begin a list of things that make you happy. Only include those items that are gifts from God.

- As time passes, add to the list.

- When you feel challenged, review the list and embrace the gifts in your life.

9.   **Make faith a daily part of your journey**
- Create a virtual shoebox. When you are hurting, pray.

Take the one item that is causing the most pain and give it up to God. Put it in the shoebox, and place the box on a high closet shelf. Only touch the shoebox to put another pain or worry inside. Never, under any circumstance, take something back out of the box.

- Find meaningful ways to connect with your faith, such as daily prayers, personal Bible lessons and group Bible studies.

- Go on walks with God for quiet time, prayer and meditation.

10.   Define your circle of support and strategic alliances

- List all of the people who have been true, genuine and supportive as you have dealt with betrayal.

- Accept that not everyone you once considered a close friend will be on the list.

- Create a list of strategic alliances, including doctors, therapists, organizations and Internet resources.

- Keep these lists handy for reference.

11.   Face the details with eyes wide open

- Learn as much as you can about your specific betrayal.

- Find out more about that type of crime or betrayal in general, so you can find resources to help you and avoid similar circumstances in the future.

- Reach out to others in your same situation.

- Speak out.

12.   Lists and letters

- Create a list of unknowns.

- Categorize each unknown as something you can or cannot control.

- Check off each item as it reaches "known" status.

- Write a letter to your betrayer, detailing your frustrations, anger, thoughts and hurts.

- Destroy the letter.

- Again, find ways to speak out.

13.   H.E.A.L to be Real

- Hug and touch.

- Exercise and eat healthy.

- Ask for – and accept – help.

- Laugh and smile a lot.

APPENDIX – B

RESOURCES FOR PROTECTING CHILDREN

These organizations and web sites can help parents, grandparents and educators detect predators in children's lives. What's more, the information provided by these incredible groups can help you devise strategies to communicate with, empower and protect children.

Dallas Children's Advocacy Center
(214) 818-2600
www.dcac.org

Enough is Enough – ProtectKids.com
www.protectkids.com

Family Watchdog – National Sex Offender Registry
www.familywatchdog.us

Federal Bureau of Investigation – Crimes Against Children program
www.fbi.gov/hq/cid/cac/crimesmain.htm

**National Association to Prevent Sexual Abuse
of Children**
(651) 340-0537
www.napsac.us

National Center for Missing & Exploited Children
(703) 274-3900
(800) 843-5678
www.missingkids.com

National Children's Advocacy Center
(256) 533-KIDS (5437)
www.nationalcac.org

National Academy of Sciences – Net Safe Kids
www.nap.edu/netsafekids

NetSmartz
www.NetSmartz.org

APPENDIX – C

BIBLIOGRAPHY

Baptiste, Baron, and Richard Corman. Journey into Power: How to Sculpt Your Ideal Body, Free Your True Self, and Transform Your Life with Yoga. New York: Fireside, 2003.

"Child Protection Tips." LifeTips.com. LifeTips.com, Inc. 2 Nov. 2008. <http://childprotection.lifetips.com/cat/63584/child-predators/>.

"Child Safety." National Center for Missing & Exploited Children. National Center for Missing & Exploited Children. 2 Nov. 2008. <http://www.missingkids.com/missingkids/servlet/pageservlet?languagecountry=en_us&pageid=713>.

Davis, Rachel, Lisa F. Parks, and Larry Cohen. Sexual Violence and the Spectrum of Prevention: Towards a Community Solution. Rep. No. National Sexual Violence Resource Center. National Sexual Violence Resource Center, 2006.

Diagnostic and Statistical Manual of Mental Disorders : DSM-IV. New York:American Psychiatric, Incorporated, 1994.

"Education: Tools & Resources." Dallas Children's Advocacy Center. Dallas Children's Advocacy Center. 15 Oct. 2008. <http://www.dcac.org/pages/education_resources.aspx>.

Eichenwald, Kurt. "Dark Corners: From Their Own Online World, Pedophiles Extend Their Reach." The New York Times, 21 Aug. 2006.

Jakes, T.D. Mama Made the Difference : Life Lessons My Mother Taught Me. London: Turnaround Publisher Services Limited, 2006.

Kubler-Ross, Elisabeth. On Death and Dying. New York: Scribner, 1997.

Lanning, Kenneth V. Child Molesters: A Behavioral Analysis. Federal Bureau of Investigation. Fourth ed. Alexandria, VA: National Center for Missing & Exploited Children, 2001.

"North American Man/Boy Love Association." Wikipedia. 4 Feb. 2006. <http://en.wikipedia.org/wiki/nambla>.

A Parent's Guide to Internet Safety. Crimes Against Children. Federal Bureau of Investigation. 31 Mar. 2006. <http://www. fbi.gov/publications/pguide/pguidee.htm>.

Ruggles, Tammy L. "Profile of a Pedophile." Mental Health Matters. 15 Apr. 2005 <http://www.mental-health-matters. com/articles/article.php?artid=273>.

Ruiz, Don Miguel. The Mastery of Love: A Practical Guide to the Art of Relationships. Grand Rapids: Amber-Allen, Incorporated, 1999.

Salter, Anna. Predators : Pedophiles, Rapists, and Other Sex Offenders: Who They Are, How They Operate, and How We Can Protect Ourselves and Our Children. New York: Basic Books, 2004.

Temple, Dinah S. Picking up the Pieces. Bloomington: Authorhouse, 2004.

Tolle, Eckhart. The Power of Now: A Guide to Spiritual Enlightenment. Chicago: New World Library, 2004.

Yamada, Kobi. She. Grand Rapids: Compendium, Incorporated, & Communications, 2004.

ACKNOWLEDGEMENTS

During this journey, many wonderful people have touched this project and our lives. This book lived inside me for more than three years. Yet for the courage to put it on paper, I needed a community of friends, family and talented experts. I am eternally grateful for each and every one of you.

Cynthia Stine has been a tremendous asset, as both a phenomenal publicist and genuine friend. Thank you for helping create the opportunities to speak out on such an important topic. Lesley Hensell provided her unique gifts as an editor, working tirelessly and passionately to create a final manuscript of which I am so proud. Thanks to Joshua Surgeon for sharing his special talents of layout and design. I extend deep appreciation to my very creative friends, Kim Schlossberg and Kathleen Wilke, for sharing their talents as well.

Profound thanks to Special Agent Michael Call of the Federal Bureau of Investigation for doing his job brilliantly while also sensitively dealing with my children and me, the secondary victims in this tragedy.

Several amazing individuals helped me grow comfortable writing our story and sharing my personal steps of healing. My appreciation to the talented freelance writer Trey Garrison, who provided my first safe haven to speak out about child predators. My gratitude also goes to Lynn Davis, Ellen Magnis, Anne Ferguson and a multitude of other friends at Dallas Children's Advocacy Center (DCAC) for allowing me to be part of an educational outreach program that is second-to-none. DCAC's umbrella approach to working with victims of child abuse has served as an ideal model for this book. I am indebted to Oprah Winfrey and her producers, who empowered me to reach a broad audience as the show passionately took on NAMBLA and child predators. Together, I hope we were able to both educate parents and save the lives of children.

I am fortunate to work in an environment where my co-workers are truly my friends. Special thanks to everyone at Professional Bank for their support, patience and friendship as I worked on this project.

In my circle of friends and family, I first must thank Bill Fountain, a talented author and friend, for encouraging me to put my story on paper. Another dear friend and gifted author, Julie Lenzer Kirk, provided guidance, tips of the trade, and the support I needed when I was ready to give up. While I cannot name them all here, the children and I are filled with thanks to the countless friends and family who have provided shoulders to cry on, hugs, emails, cards, trays of food, help with carpooling, and so much encouragement for me to write this book as a part of my own therapeutic process. A special note of thanks to Father John, Deacon Ken and our faith community, whose guidance, prayers and support were often what kept us going during our dark days.

Michelle, if I had a wish to give to the world, it would be that every person could have a friend like you. Your love is unconditional; your patience is never-ending. Thank you for choosing me as your friend. Thank you for being a second mom to my kids. Thank you for sharing in both the tears and the laughter encountered throughout this journey.

Buddy and Renee, Debbie and Sergio, thank you all for your love as my siblings and sibling-in-laws. You have stood by me and the children in our darkest times, and I am deeply blessed to have you all so near and dear. I attribute a large part of the kids' healing to the family that consistently surrounded us and held us up.

I would not be the woman I am today without the love, guidance and lessons from my precious Mom and Dad, Jeanne and Bud. There are no words to describe all you have done to help me reach this moment, so I will inadequately just say, "thank you." I am the result of your love, hardships and blessings, and I am so proud to be your daughter.

Scott, God knew what he was doing when he brought you into my life in 2006. Thank you for loving me, loving my children, and being there for us through so many difficult moments in our healing. You are my angel. Even though it took four decades to find you, you were worth the wait. I look forward to the next four decades as your adoring wife.

Austin and Alexa, thank you for your unconditional love, your patience and your faith in me, your Mom. People often ask if I wish I could just erase all the bad stuff and bad people from my life. My answer is always, without hesitation, "absolutely not!" I could never erase my past, because you are the beautiful blessings that came from it. Thank you for all the gifts you have given me—every hug, reminding me to go with the flow, your smiles and laughter, and the pure joy of being your Mom. This is *our* story, *our* journey of recovery and *our* catalyst to a beautiful life ahead. I love you both!

About the Author

Darlene Ellison's gripping personal story forms the foundation of her High-Touch Alliances and Betrayal Recovery concepts, which she uses to inspire and compel audiences into changing their own lives.

Ellison's expertise in overcoming obstacles is best illustrated by her personal fight against child predators. In her efforts to teach parents, grandparents and caregivers about the dangers of child predators, Ellison has been featured on *The Oprah Winfrey Show*, *20/20* and *Dateline NBC*, as well as in Dallas' *D Magazine*. In addition, Ellison has appeared in parent education videos for the Catholic Diocese of Dallas' Safe Environment Plan and Dallas Children's Advocacy Center.

Professionally, Ellison serves as vice president of business development for Professional Bank, N.A., allowing her to create a unique business-development strategic plan that focuses on niche positioning and high-touch customer service. She is founder and coordinator of two award-winning community Women In Business organizations, which help women business owners and executives grow personally and professionally. As an extension of these programs, Ellison also has created the Future Women in Business internship program for college-aged women.

Ellison also works as a consultant on overcoming obstacles and building meaningful alliances. To that end, she offers speaking services, workshops and executive retreats to help businesses, organizations and associations transform and empower employees and members with her empowering and inspiring presentations. Ellison's strategies are bolstered by her professional background, which includes working as a development consultant for various non-profit organizations, as well as working in private practice as a licensed psychology associate. Ellison earned a bachelor's degree in business from Southern Methodist University and a master's degree in psychology from Texas A&M University – Commerce.

Darlene lives in Dallas with her husband, Scott, and two thriving teenagers.

DISCARD